D1433744

ase return or

NATHAN OUTLAW'S EVERYDAY SEAFOOD

Hardie Grant

QUADRILLE

Foreword

It's a great honour to write the foreword for this beautiful book, especially as one of the best meals I've had this year was at Nathan's restaurant in Port Isaac. I've only known Nathan for the past few years, but boy is he an infectious soul. He's a massive softie with a big heart and one of the nicest guys in the restaurant industry. Our dads are both chefs, and that's probably what's given us the same level of pride for how we behave within the industry, as well as instilling in us an approach to recipe writing that ensures cooking is inclusive and accessible.

That is exactly what Nathan has achieved in this gorgeous book. His honest and uncomplicated approach speaks volumes in these pages. He's a tall boy with a big presence, but his food is beautifully delicate, thoughtfully presented, and at its core embraces simple, clean, balanced flavours.

For me, this is a real genre buster of a book. Often people are nervous about cooking with seafood, but there's no need to be. On these pages you'll find incredible, modern and exciting dishes, and totally doable techniques that will serve you well for the rest of your life. Read through all the handy up-front info to get you in the right spirit, then pick your recipes and get cooking.

Mr Outlaw certainly isn't messing about, and as well as everything looking and sounding phenomenal, he's definitely got all the bases covered. From some of the quickest most delicate raw dishes – which I think are my favourites – to twists on the classics, such as Crab Scotch quail's eggs or Cod and ox cheek stew. Most are super economical if you're buying seasonally, then there's a few things that are a bit naughtier – Barbecued jerk lobster with coconut rice I'm looking at you! There's a whole lot to choose from.

Without doubt, Nathan is one of Britain's most devoted chefs, but because we like to pigeonhole people we think that he's only about seafood, and although he probably would have married a mermaid should he have had access to one, the desserts in this book are totally delicious, too.

Finally, in crafting this book, Nathan has worked with the lovely David Loftus, one of the best food photographers on the planet and another of my favourite people in the industry, so you can be sure that every photo will inspire you in an instant.

Nice one mate.
Jamie Oliver

Introduction

Seafood is the best convenience food ever! That's a bold statement, but it's true. Most seafood will cook within minutes – much faster than any ready prepared meal – and that, for me, is what makes it such a great choice for everyday meal occasions. I wanted to write this book to unlock the myth that seafood is a tricky thing to deal with: it's not. Follow my recipes and you will realise just how easy it is to cook.

Each recipe has been tested to make sure it can be cooked successfully at home – taking into account timing, availability of ingredients and the equipment needed. I've done this personally, so I know the recipes work and that you'll be able to follow them easily. The biggest single piece of advice I can give you is to read through the method before you start to cook, especially with the slightly more ambitious dishes.

The recipes are a collection of my take on classics from far and wide, with the simple approach to seafood that I'm known for. I've made sure the ingredients are accessible and can be bought easily because I don't want you to be put off by long lists of unfamiliar items.

However, the most significant point about the ingredients is that all the fish and shellfish used in these recipes is sustainable at the time of writing. The importance of sustainability is something I cannot stress enough. Please ask questions when you are buying. Any fishmonger or supplier worth your custom will have an acute awareness of sustainability and know where their seafood has come from. If they can't answer your questions, don't buy from them.

Once you become more confident, I hope you'll treat my recipes as a guide rather than stick to them. Feel free to play around with different fish and flavourings. It gives me such pride and pleasure when someone tells me they've tried a recipe from my book and then cooked it differently next time, adding this or that, and it tasted just as good... or better!

The recipes can be scaled up or down to suit your needs, so don't be put off if a recipe serves four and there's just two of you. Just halve the quantities, or double or triple them for a crowd. It will be fine.

And finally, although this book will look lovely on your coffee table, I would much rather see it in the kitchen covered in splatters of food. I've written it to be used, so please go ahead... and enjoy!

Why eat fish and shellfish?

Apart from the fact that very fresh seafood tastes wonderful, there are many health benefits. Current guidelines suggest that we should eat at least two portions of fish a week. Not enough if you ask me! Fish is an excellent source of protein, vitamins and minerals. Oily fish has the significant added bonus of being rich in omega-3 fatty acids, which help to keep our heart, joints, skin and eyes healthy. And some of the smaller oily fish can be eaten whole, so they provide a particularly rich source of calcium and phosphorus.

For those who need to follow a low fat diet, the obvious choice is white fish, although not cooked in batter or breadcrumbs. Shellfish is also low in fat and a good source of zinc, iodine, copper and selenium. Mussels, oysters and crab provide a fair amount of omega-3 fatty acids too.

However, we need to set a few limits on the amount of oily fish we consume as they sometimes contain low levels of pollutants, which can build up in the body. It is suggested that we should eat no more than four portions of oily fish per week. For anyone who is pregnant or breastfeeding, this reduces to two portions per week.

Bream, bass, turbot and brown crabmeat may also contain low levels of pollutants so it makes sense to eat these in moderation too. Swordfish is not featured in my book, but I should warn you that it can contain significant levels of mercury and should be restricted to a maximum of two portions per week. Anyone who is pregnant or breastfeeding should avoid swordfish altogether.

You are now forewarned! But I doubt whether any of you are planning to eat fish at every meal so these issues are unlikely to be a problem.

Buying and storing seafood

It goes without saying that you should buy the freshest fish available to you. It could be that you are lucky enough to have a 'proper' fishmonger on your doorstep, or maybe even access to the fishermen themselves. If not, you will find that some of the better supermarkets now employ trained staff on their fish counters, so don't be reticent to buy from them. Remember to take a cool bag with you to bring the fish home in; it will keep that much fresher.

Always take a look around the place you're buying from. Make sure it's clean and that the fish is displayed well. Also check out those behind the counter. They should be confident and handle their fish and shellfish cleanly and carefully. And they must be able to answer any questions you have about the fish they are selling. If they can't, it's best to give the place a wide berth.

All fish and seafood should smell of the ozone rather than 'fishy'. If it smells at all unpleasant, don't buy it! Make sure that whole fish look good. They should be intact with no visible damage to any part. Eyes should be bright and clear, gills should be vivid red, and any scales that you expect to be there should be in place. Flat fish should be firm and have some sea slime on the surface. Oily fish should have retained their natural colour and be vibrant, not dull.

In the case of shellfish, you will also need to check on their status. Molluscs need to be alive when you buy them. If clams, cockles, mussels or oysters have open shells, tap them firmly and if they don't close readily, don't buy as this indicates that the shellfish are no longer alive.

One exception to the 'live' rule is scallops, which often come to the market ready prepared and cut from the shell. However, they should still smell ozony and sweet. Also, make sure they are firm and haven't been left to soak. If any of these criteria aren't met, leave them in the shop!

When buying lobsters and crabs, again, they should be alive. Check there are no bubbles coming from their mouths as this is a sign that they are stressed and it will affect the quality of their meat. Lobsters should have long antennae; short ones suggest the lobster has been stored for a long while and has either begun to eat itself or been eaten by others.

Finally, the cephalopods – squid, octopus and cuttlefish – really need to be eaten within a couple of days of being caught. Their eyes should be bright and the creatures should be intact, with no signs of changing colour to pink, as this suggests they have seen better days.

If you've found a bargain or someone has brought you lots of freshly caught fish, don't turn it away – most fish freezes well.

Ideally, seafood should be eaten within 24 hours of buying. Store it wrapped in a damp cloth in the coldest area of the fridge. Don't let it sit in water though, as this will impair the flavour. The fridge needs to be between 0°C and 2°C. If you can, cover the wrapped fish with a layer of fresh ice – don't let it touch the fish directly as this will cause 'freezer burn'. Stored carefully on the bone, most fish will be fine for several days.

If you know that you won't be eating the fish within a few days, take it off the bone, make sure it's completely dry, then place it in a freezerproof container using greaseproof paper to separate portions if necessary and put it in the freezer as soon as you can. It will keep quite happily for up to 2 months. In the case of lobster and crab, cook and cool before freezing in the same way as for fish. Always allow fish and seafood to defrost slowly in the fridge before cooking.

Fish prep tools and equipment

Buying equipment for cooking can be daunting – there's so much out there to choose from. I've put together a list of the items I use day in, day out and have been using for the last twenty years. Remember though, this is my personal choice and you may already have, or prefer to buy, something different. That's fine, but please make sure you buy good quality products. Trust me, if you skimp, you'll only be buying again soon, which is not only frustrating, it can end up costing you more…

Knives

I strongly recommend investing in a selection of good knives for your kitchen. The following are the ones I use all the time:

Filleting knife There are many types of filleting knife on the market, with various uses. I use a thin, semi-flexible bladed one. You can get some that are very flexible but they are not easy to sharpen. If you buy a good quality filleting knife, it should last a lifetime.

Cook's knife I tend to use two cook's knives. One has a 25cm long blade. The other is heavier with a 30cm blade – it needs to be because I use it for bashing lobsters and crabs and steaking fish. It's much safer to use a heavy knife for jobs like this so that it doesn't bounce off and injure you. I use the lighter 25cm knife for slicing and chopping, and I keep the blade razor sharp.

Paring knife A good paring knife is a must. Don't be tempted to buy one that's too big or you'll find it clumsy to handle, when you are peeling garlic or an onion for example. Keep it nice and sharp at all times. Apart from preparing veg and fruit, I also use a small paring knife for scaling fish, but do be careful if you try this – It's much safer to use a proper fish scaler.

Serrated knife A strong serrated knife is most useful for cutting off fish heads. When I'm dealing with bigger fish, I always cut the head off first as I find it gives you more control when filleting.

Oyster knife It took me years to find an oyster knife that I like to use. The one I own and love has a wooden handle and a firm but short blade. I always keep it sharpened so it slices through the muscle cleanly, giving a very presentable oyster.

Firm bladed boning knife This is a personal preference and technically not a correct use of this knife but I find a boning knife is the best one to use for opening scallops. If you're planning to open lots of scallops, I'd suggest investing in one.

Sharpener

I've always been terrible at keeping my knives sharp. It's not the most interesting of jobs to do in the kitchen. However, I had a revelation when I discovered a sharpener with a guided sharpening wheel on it. I'm not really one for gadgets but since I've been using this, my knives are always sharp and ready to rock. A great investment!

Rubber mallet

I always use a rubber mallet when I want to steak fish into portions.

Hitting the heavy 30cm cook's knife with the mallet leaves you with a very clean and precise cut.

Microplane grater

This is probably one of the most frequently used pieces of kit in my kitchen. These graters are worth every penny and if looked after properly should last you for ages. We use them for zesting citrus fruit and grating cheese, garlic, chocolate, etc. Trust me, once you begin using one, it will become an integral part of your life in the kitchen. One word of warning though: they are very sharp, so mind your fingers!

Mandoline

A Japanese mandoline is a good friend to have in your kitchen. I use one a lot for finely slicing vegetables, such as fennel, for salads and pickles. Again, be very careful. Fingers and mandolines don't mix!

Thin-handled dessertspoon

This has a few, important functions. Firstly, it's ideal for scooping a scallop out of its shell because the bowl is made of thin, rounded metal, almost the same shape as the rounded side of a scallop shell. Secondly, I use it when picking crabs. Using both handle and bowl ends, these spoons can get into every crevice of a crab shell, enabling me to prise out every last piece of that fantastic crabmeat. Also, they tend not to break the cartilage too much, and you don't want that in your crabmeat. Of course, these spoons are also useful for tasting as you cook, and for serving up when you are aiming to get the presentation precise.

Pin-boning tweezers

These are an absolutely essential item for your fish prepping kit. Make sure you buy a pair that have no flex to them. The flexible ones seem to struggle to grab smaller bones.

Chopping boards

It is worth investing in a good quality blue plastic chopping board if you plan to do lots of fish prep. When you have finished using it, always wash the board with cold water rather than hot, as hot water will cook the remaining debris and make the board smell.

Always dry the board thoroughly before putting it away too, as again it will smell if you don't.

For other food prep, I love using my large wooden chopping boards, but I really wouldn't recommend wood for preparing fish, as it is very difficult to clean the fish debris from. Never, ever be tempted to put your wooden chopping board into the dishwasher as it does very strange things to them!

Small stainless steel bowls

These are not expensive to buy but they are so useful to have to hand for all sorts of purposes, from holding pre-prepped ingredients to mixing small quantities of dressing and storing food in the fridge. Get several – you'll be reaching for them all the time!

Sieves

I would recommend having a choice of sieves in your kitchen. It just makes it easier to achieve the desired result.

A fine sieve is best for sauces and stocks. A slightly coarser sieve is great for purées and breadcrumbs. A large conical strainer is useful for straining fish stocks.

Heat resistant spatula

A good quality flexible, heatproof rubber spatula is a great kitchen tool. Ideal for mixing, it gets right into the edges of the pan or bowl you're using, and enables you to scrape out every last bit when you have finished.

Electronic digital scales

Having electronic digital scales to hand in your kitchen makes life that much easier. Try to get scales that have a decent sized platform and weigh in metric and imperial for both dry goods and liquids. Take care of them though. They are quite delicate and feature at the top of our 'Chef, the equipment is broken' list!

Electric blender/processor

Once again, it pays long term to buy robust, good quality small electrical appliances. If you want soups and purées that are really fine, a powerful electric blender or food processor is a must. Always be careful when putting hot liquid into a blender though, as the machine has a tendency to throw the liquid up at you as hot air builds up.

Electric mixer

I don't often use my mixer when I'm preparing fish, but it's really handy for puddings. If you do buy one, choose one that is of good quality and comes with all the attachments you are likely to need. It's worth paying a bit more for something that will last.

Pans

There are loads of pans on the market but if you want a really good long-term investment, choose the ones

with heavy bottoms and tight-fitting lids. If they're ovenproof, even better. A thicker bottomed pan helps cook food more evenly and gives you lots of residual heat when you take it off the heat source. They are also good to braise in, hence the need for a tight-fitting lid.

For pan-frying fish, a good quality non-stick pan is essential as far as I'm concerned. You need to look after it though. Don't leave it on the heat as you might a cast iron pan. If you do, after a while the coating will burn off... you really don't want bits of non-stick coating in your food.

Oven and grill trays

Whether you are grilling or baking, you need to invest in some good quality trays. If they are too thin, they'll buckle under the heat and the food won't cook evenly. Buy a range of sizes – from trays big enough to hold a couple of fish fillets up to one big enough to take a whole fish. If you buy cast iron, make sure that you dry them well after washing or they will go rusty. A little tip: I always wash and dry my trays then finish them in a warm oven to make sure they are thoroughly dry.

Steamer

Steaming fish shows off the freshness of the fish and the purity of its flavour. It's one of my favourite ways to cook fish. A steamer is a great piece of kit and worth every penny. If you're very fortunate you may have an integrated steamer in your oven. Otherwise, you can buy one to use on the hob. You might choose to get one of the tall electric steamers, but I prefer to use a simple metal steamer.

A word on cling film

Please avoid using cling film and instead use inverted plates, greaseproof paper or reusable plastic containers.

Pairing wine with seafood

Damon Little, Sommelier, Outlaw's New Road

There's nothing better than discovering a sensational new wine – one that ticks all the boxes, and every sip is absolute bliss. If it's then paired successfully to a recipe the pleasure is heightened even further.

If you are feeling a little adventurous and fancy trying something new, consider buying wine from an independent wine merchant. Often the people who work there will have tasted most of the wines on offer and will be able to give you sound advice and make suitable suggestions.

Higher price does not necessarily indicate better quality wine, as you may be buying a very expensive wine that is not ready to drink and could therefore be rather unpleasant. Having said that, please be aware that if you purchase a wine for £5 almost half of that goes towards excise and duty, leaving wine that is, in reality, worth approximately £2.50. Deduct VAT, the cost of the bottle, transport, the retailer's mark-up and the producer's mark-up and eventually the liquid in the bottle is worth only a few pennies... Are you really going to enjoy that?

If you are not sure where to begin when it comes to choosing wine to drink with seafood, my advice would be to start by having your favourite wine with your favourite recipe. You'll get to know which combinations are pleasurable and which are not so good. Most of us would taste the wine before eating, so sip the wine again after a mouthful of food and see how the food affects the wine and vice versa.

There are many, if not hundreds, of wines that work well with seafood beyond the familiar classic partners, such as Muscadet or Champagne with freshly shucked oysters. The most successful pairings occur when the structure of the wine works in harmony with the structure of the recipe. The structure of wine can be broken down into body and flavour intensity, acidity and sweetness.

Body and flavour intensity

A bold dish requires a bold wine. The most practical way to determine the body of a wine is to compare the mouth-feel to that of water, milk or cream, which would translate to light, medium and full bodied. Match the textures of your recipe with the body of your wine. If the dish is bold then the flavours of wine should be bold.

Acidity

You can determine the level of acidity in wine by assessing the effect on salivation. The next time you taste white wine, tilt your head forward and down with your lips closed to ascertain how much saliva builds up in your mouth. Acidity in wine is detected towards the back and at the sides of your tongue. Acidity in wine pairs well with fatty or oily foods, as it has a palate-cleansing 'cutting through' effect, which counteracts the richness of the food. Note that acidity in food reduces the effect of acidity in wine.

Sweetness

This an incredibly objective aspect of wine. You may have a dry aromatic wine offering flavours of ripe peaches and apricots, which in our minds resembles sweetness, yet it is still a dry wine based on actual residual sugar. The sweetness level in wine is detected at the very tip of your tongue.

Sweet food reduces the sweetness in wine, so the sweetness in wine should either be equal or preferably a little higher than that of the dish. Sweetness in wine is also a fantastic complement to salty food, so a sweet wine works with blue cheese. Try Sauternes with Roquefort. It's amazing!

Other characteristics

Be aware that the bitterness in food increases the bitterness in wine. Also, heat generated from chilli can increase the perception of bitterness, astringency and acidity – and you will also feel the heat from the alcohol causing a slight burn.

Red wine with fish?

We have had many successful red wine pairings with seafood. There are numerous low tannin light bodied reds available. The reason those reds have a lighter body and lighter tannic structure is because the actual skin of the grape is much thinner than others. For example, Gamay and Pinot Noir will be lighter than Cabernet Sauvignon and Merlot. One of the most sensational combinations is salmon and beetroot with an earthy, spicy Pinot Noir that has good acidity.

Wine and seafood varieties

When choosing wine, you need to consider the different characteristics of fish and shellfish varieties.

Flat white fish: Dover sole, lemon sole, plaice, megrim, witch, turbot, brill, rays
These range in density, but generally have a light flavour. Minerality is key when choosing your matching wine. For the lighter style of flat fish like sole or plaice, pair floral wines that offer orchard fruit (apple/pear). Of course, hints of citrus are an advantage too.

Round white fish: bream, cod, gurnard, haddock, hake, John Dory, ling, monkfish, whiting
These have slightly more flavour than flat white fish, but pair well with similar wines. Wines with hints of citrus and orchard fruit work best.

White fish with slightly oily flesh: grey mullet, red mullet, bass
Wines produced on marl (marine fossil soil), such as Jura wines, complement the subtle earthiness of these fish, but acidity is of the essence here to cut through the oiliness of the fish.

Oily fish: mackerel, sardine, herring, salmon, sea trout
These stronger flavoured fish call for aromatic wines with higher acidity to cut through their oiliness. Alsace wines are good options, especially Riesling. Avoid red wine with tannins as it may cause a metallic reaction.

Cephalopods: squid, octopus, cuttles
These have a delicate flavour and a soft texture. The light, white pepperiness of Grüner Veltliner backed up by the hints of soft stone fruit work particularly well with cephalopods.

Molluscs: clams, razor clams, cockles, mussels, oysters
As these are high in minerals, avoid serving red wines with tannins, as it may cause a metallic reaction. The ultimate pairings include Champagne, Chablis and Muscadet, all of which are crisp, zingy and mineral.

Shellfish: scallops, crab, lobster
These are usually cooked with butter, or have a buttery sauce or dressing, so fuller bodied, buttery wines are an excellent choice. Try a white Burgundy from the Côte de Beaune. Very fresh shellfish has an underlying sweetness, which could be complemented by an off-dry style of wine, or a crisp, aromatic Albariño from Galicia, Spain; Gisborne from Eastland, New Zealand; or Montevideo from Uruguay.

There may be several different fish and shellfish within a dish, plus vegetables, fruit, etc. to consider when you are choosing a wine. As a guideline, try and match the flavour of your wine to the strongest flavour of the dish, but consider how it will pair with the mildest flavour too.

Planning a fish menu

Sometimes it's hard to know what to cook and even more so when you have constraints on your time, or a party to cater for. Getting everything to balance in terms of flavours, textures and effort involved takes some practice so I've decided to give you a few pointers by suggesting five menus for different occasions using the recipes from the book. Scale the quantities up or down, according to the number you are serving, and add your own choice of veg, salad and bread where necessary.

A quick dinner for two

You can rustle this up in less than an hour – perfect for a midweek after-work supper.

Smoked Mackerel & Pickled Vegetable Salad (page 141)
Haddock Baked in a Bag with Béarnaise Butter (page 152)
Pear Crumble with Earl Grey Chocolate Sauce (page 200)

A leisurely lunch for four

An ideal meal to serve when lunch can extend through the afternoon, or supper can go on through the evening, taking time between courses to chat and raise a glass.

Raw Salmon with Vodka, Orange & Horseradish (page 48)
Soused Gurnard, Red Pepper Ketchup, Rocket & Olive Salad (page 79)
Lemon Sole, Green Sauce Butter (page 177)
Rhubarb Sponge, Almond Cream & Lemon Crème Fraîche (page 198)

A dinner to impress for six or more

For a special occasion, it's always good to come up with a menu that leaves you little to do at the last minute. This one works a treat.

Crab Scotch Quail's Eggs with Watercress Mayonnaise (page 22)
Gin-cured Sea Trout with Apple & Fennel (page 56)
Dressed Lobster with Herb Mayonnaise (page 128)
Cod & Ox Cheek Stew (page 114)
Warm Chocolate Tart 'Black Pig' (page 203)

Outdoor summer meal for six or more

As far as I'm concerned, there's only one way to cook on a hot day – outside on the barbecue. Add a couple of salads, a pudding and a few drinks, relax and enjoy!

Prawn, Chilli & Potato Salad (page 126)
Monkfish, Cauliflower Pickle, Ginger & Coriander Yoghurt (page 188)
Mackerel with Barbecue Sauce (page 190)
Gurnard with Fennel, Gherkin & Olive Salad (page 194)
Elderflower Cream with Strawberry Sorbet (page 205)

A family buffet for eight to ten

For a buffet you need dishes that will happily sit on the table for a while, so it's easier if most of them are served at room temperature. I like to include a couple that can be warmed up easily too.

Prawn Cocktail Quiche (page 26)
Hot-smoked Salmon Pâté, Whisky Jelly (page 32)
Jacob's Favourite Cod's Roe Dip (page 34)
Doom Bar Marinated Seafood (page 69)
Crab & Tomato Salad with Horseradish Dressing (page 124)
Sardine, Pepper & Shallot Flatbreads (page 156)
Treacle & Raspberry Tart (page 210)

STARTERS & SMALL BITES

For this beautiful starter, make sure your crabmeat is in tip-top condition, as the dish really shows off its quality. Trust me, you will get a few wows when your guests, family and friends try it. I like to serve it with a pile of lightly toasted sourdough.

Crab pâté with pink grapefruit

Serves 4 as a starter
300g white crabmeat (from
 a 1.5kg freshly cooked crab)
Sea salt and freshly ground
 black pepper

For the pâté
200g brown crabmeat, sieved
1½ sheets of bronze leaf
 gelatine
30ml brandy
A pinch of cayenne pepper
A pinch of ground cumin
200ml double cream
2 tbsp lime juice

For the pink grapefruit jelly
2½ sheets of bronze leaf
 gelatine
300ml freshly squeezed pink
 grapefruit juice (from about
 2 grapefruit)
50g caster sugar
A pinch of sea salt

To garnish
1 pink grapefruit, segmented
Mustard cress
A drizzle of olive oil

To serve
Sourdough bread

Pick through your crabmeat, checking for any shell or cartilage to discard. Put the white crabmeat into a bowl and season with salt and pepper to taste. Put 4 tbsp into a small bowl for the garnish and refrigerate. Divide the rest equally between 4 small bowls or ramekins.

To make the pâté, soak the gelatine in a shallow dish of ice-cold water for about 5 minutes to soften. Heat the brown crabmeat, brandy and spices in a small pan over a low heat. Simmer gently for a minute, then add the cream and heat through.

Remove the gelatine from the dish and squeeze out the excess water, then add it to the brown crab, off the heat, stirring to melt. Transfer to a blender and blend for 1 minute, adding the lime juice and a pinch of salt. Pass the mixture through a sieve into a jug and pour it equally over the white crabmeat in the bowls. Place in the fridge to set.

While the crab pâté is setting, make the grapefruit jelly. Soak the gelatine in ice-cold water, as above, to soften. Put the grapefruit juice, sugar and a pinch of salt into a pan and bring to the boil. Remove the gelatine from the dish and squeeze out the excess water, then add to the juice mixture, off the heat, stirring until fully melted. Leave to cool, but don't let it set.

When the pâté is set, pour the cooled, liquid jelly evenly over the surface and return to the fridge to set.

Take the pâté out of the fridge around 20 minutes before serving to bring it to room temperature. Cut away the peel and pith from the grapefruit and cut out the segments from between the membranes; cut these into smaller pieces.

To serve, spoon the reserved white crabmeat on top of the pâté. Add the grapefruit pieces, scatter over some cress and drizzle with olive oil. Toast the sourdough and serve with the pâté.

Okay, so these little nibbles are not real Scotch eggs, but they are just as tasty in my opinion, and they work so well with the peppery watercress mayonnaise. If the idea of crab doesn't float your boat, we do a fabulous smoked fish version too – just replace the crab with smoked haddock and proceed in the same way.

Crab Scotch quail's eggs with watercress mayonnaise

**Makes 12; Serves 4
as a starter**

For the crab mix
200g fresh cod fillet, diced
75g brown crabmeat, sieved
200g white crabmeat, picked
Finely grated zest of 1 lemon
2 tbsp chopped chives
Sea salt and freshly ground
  black pepper

For the eggs
14 quail's eggs (includes
  2 extras in case of breakage)
100g plain flour, for coating
2 medium (hen's) eggs,
  beaten
100g day-old bread, blitzed in
  a blender to crumbs
Sunflower oil for deep-frying

For the watercress
  mayonnaise
2 egg yolks
¾ tsp English mustard
20g mature Cheddar, grated
1½ tbsp white wine vinegar
3 tbsp watercress, chopped
300ml sunflower oil

To serve
1 lemon, cut into wedges

Put the cod fillet into a food processor with a good pinch of salt and blend for 30 seconds. Add the brown crabmeat and blend for a further 30 seconds. Scrape into a bowl and add the white crabmeat, lemon zest, chives and seasoning. Mix together well, cover and place in the fridge.

Place the quail's eggs in a pan, cover with cold water and bring to the boil over a high heat. Meanwhile, get ready a bowl of ice-cold water. As soon as the water begins to boil, take the eggs out of the pan and plunge them into the ice-cold water. Let cool, then peel the eggs.

Set up three bowls: one with flour, one with beaten eggs and one with breadcrumbs. Using clean hands, carefully mould the crab mixture around each quail's egg and pass through the flour, then the egg and finally the breadcrumbs to coat. Put the eggs to one side, or in the fridge if you are cooking them later.

To make the mayonnaise, put the egg yolks into a blender or small food processor with the mustard, grated cheese, wine vinegar and watercress. Process for 1 minute and then, with the motor still running, slowly pour in the oil. Once it is fully emulsified, stop the machine and season the mayonnaise with salt to taste. Transfer to a bowl, cover and refrigerate.

When ready to serve, heat the oil in a deep-fat fryer or other suitable deep, heavy pan to 160°C. Deep-fry the Scotch eggs in the hot oil, in batches as necessary, for about 3 minutes until golden. Drain on kitchen paper and season with a little salt.

Spoon the watercress mayonnaise into a bowl. Place the Scotch eggs on a warm platter with the bowl of mayonnaise and lemon wedges.

Oysters and bacon are a great flavour combination. Their salty and rich flavours need something to cut them, and that's where the zingy dipping sauce comes in – it has a little kick from the chilli too. A cucumber and fennel salad brings the whole dish together with its lovely fresh textures.

Pancetta-wrapped oyster fritters with cucumber and mint dipping sauce

Serves 4 as a starter

12 live Pacific oysters
50ml olive oil
1 white onion, peeled and finely chopped
½ fennel bulb, tough outer layer removed, finely chopped
100g fresh breadcrumbs
2 tbsp chopped mint
2 tbsp chopped curly parsley
Finely grated zest and juice of 1 lime
12 thin slices of pancetta
Sea salt and freshly ground black pepper

For the dipping sauce

1 cucumber
1 shallot, peeled and finely chopped
½ fennel bulb, tough outer layer removed, finely chopped
A small bunch of mint, leaves picked and finely sliced
1 large green chilli, deseeded and finely chopped
3 tbsp fish sauce
3 tbsp cider vinegar
3 tbsp water

For the salad

1 cucumber
1 fennel bulb, tough outer layer removed
1 tsp toasted black onion seeds
Juice of 1 lime
A generous drizzle of extra virgin olive oil

Open the oysters and strain their juice through a muslin-lined sieve into a bowl. Chop the oysters and then add them to the juices.

Heat a frying pan over a medium heat and add the olive oil. When it is hot, add the onion and fennel and cook for about 5 minutes until softened. Tip into a bowl and allow to cool slightly.

Add the oysters and juice, breadcrumbs, herbs, lime zest and juice to the softened veg and mix well. Season with pepper (you won't need salt because the oysters have enough).

Divide the mixture into 12 even-sized balls and roll them into rugby ball shapes. Lay the pancetta slices on a board and place an oyster ball on each one, then wrap in the pancetta.

Preheat your grill to its highest setting. Oil the grill pan, place the fritters on it and put to one side.

For the dipping sauce, halve, peel and deseed the cucumber, then cut into 5mm dice. Place in a bowl with all the other ingredients and toss to mix. Divide between 4 small dishes and set aside.

For the salad, halve, peel, deseed and finely slice the cucumber. Finely slice the fennel, using a mandoline if you have one. Toss the cucumber, fennel and onion seeds together, season with a little salt and dress with the lime juice and olive oil.

To cook the fritters, place them under the grill and cook for 3 minutes on one side, then carefully turn them and cook for another 3 minutes.

Divide the salad between 4 starter plates and place a dish of dipping sauce on each one. Once the fritters are cooked, divide them between the plates and serve.

I love a good prawn cocktail, who doesn't? This picnic quiche is a little nod to the 70s classic. It has the same flavours but no limp lettuce or tasteless tomato. You can make a big one if you wish, or little canapé sized ones as I sometimes do; just adjust the cooking time accordingly. Prawn cocktail will never be the same again!

Prawn cocktail quiche

Serves 6 as a starter

For the pastry
250g plain flour
150g unsalted butter, diced
1 tsp fine sea salt
2 tsp finely chopped rosemary
1 medium egg, beaten
3 tbsp milk
Egg wash (1 egg yolk beaten
  with 2 tbsp milk)

For the filling
15 raw tiger prawns, peeled,
  deveined and halved
3 medium eggs
300ml double cream
50ml good quality tomato
  ketchup, ideally homemade
  (see page 219)
½ tsp Tabasco
5 spring onions, trimmed and
  sliced
10 cherry tomatoes, halved
50g Parmesan, freshly grated
Sea salt and freshly ground
  black pepper

To make the pastry, put the flour, butter, salt and rosemary into a food processor and process until the mixture resembles fine breadcrumbs. Add the egg and milk and pulse briefly until the dough comes together. Shape the pastry into a disc, transfer to a sealed container and rest in the fridge for at least 1 hour. Preheat your oven to 190°C/Fan 175°C/Gas 5.

Roll out the pastry on a lightly floured surface to the thickness of a £1 coin and use to line a loose-based rectangular flan tin, about 25 x 10cm and 3cm deep, or an 18cm round flan tin, 3cm deep.

Line the pastry case with a sheet of greaseproof paper and add a layer of baking beans. Rest in the fridge for 15 minutes.

Bake the pastry case for 15 minutes, then lift out the paper and beans and brush the pastry with egg wash. Return to the oven for 3 minutes, then remove and set aside. Turn the oven down to 160°C/Fan 145°C/Gas 3.

For the filling, lightly beat the eggs, cream, tomato ketchup and Tabasco together and season with salt and pepper. Scatter the spring onions and cherry tomatoes in the pastry case, followed by the prawns, distributing them evenly. Pour on the egg and cream mixture, then sprinkle with the grated Parmesan. Bake for 25–30 minutes until the custard is set and the pastry is golden.

Leave the quiche in the tin on a wire rack to cool a little before slicing. Either eat warm or leave it to cool completely and take to the beach or park.

Starters and small bites

I serve these crisp-fried fish bites on cocktail sticks on a platter with a dish of chilli jam. They are great as a pre-dinner bite, or handed around at a party. Grey mullet is ideal for this sort of cooking because it has a decent oily content that stops it drying out. Mackerel, sardine and salmon are good alternatives. You'll probably have more chilli jam than you need, but it will keep for a few weeks in the fridge in a sealed container, and is delicious with cheese and cold meats.

Crispy fried grey mullet, chilli jam

**Serves 4 as a starter,
or up to 8 as a bite**

400g grey mullet fillet,
  skinned and pin-boned
2 tbsp chopped coriander
Finely grated zest of 1 lime
½ tsp ground cumin
½ tsp cayenne pepper
100g gluten-free self-raising
  flour
120ml Cornish Pilsner (or
  similar beer)
Sunflower oil for deep-frying
Sea salt and freshly ground
  black pepper

For the chilli jam

1 red onion, peeled and
  finely diced
4 red peppers, cored,
  deseeded and finely sliced
6 red chillies, deseeded and
  finely sliced
3 garlic cloves, peeled and
  chopped
400g tin plum tomatoes
300g soft brown sugar
150ml red wine vinegar
2 lemongrass stalks, tough
  outer layers removed, finely
  chopped

To serve

1 lime, cut into wedges

To make the chilli jam, put all of the ingredients into a heavy-based pan (I use a cast-iron one) and add a pinch of salt. Bring to the boil, stirring to dissolve the sugar, then lower the heat and simmer gently, stirring occasionally, for about 45 minutes until the jam is well reduced. Once it starts to catch on the bottom of the pan, stir constantly over the heat until it looks like bubbling lava. Transfer to a bowl and leave to cool. (Once cooled, the jam can be kept in the fridge in a sealed container.)

Cut the mullet into roughly 4cm chunks. Mix the chopped coriander, lime zest, cumin, cayenne and a good pinch of salt together in a bowl. Add the mullet pieces and toss to mix. Leave to marinate for 30 minutes.

To make the batter, mix the flour and beer together until smooth. Heat the oil in a deep-fat fryer or other suitable deep, heavy-based pan to 180°C. Season the fish with salt and pepper.

You will need to cook the fish in 2 or 3 batches. One at a time, dip each chunk into the batter to coat, then carefully lower into the hot oil. Deep-fry for 3–4 minutes until cooked and crispy. Gently lift the fish out and drain on kitchen paper. Keep warm while you cook the rest.

Sprinkle the fish chunks with a little salt and spear onto cocktail sticks. Serve immediately, on a platter or individual plates with a bowl of chilli jam and lime wedges on the side.

My version of the French brandade, using Cornish smoked haddock and saffron, may upset purists, but who cares – it tastes really good! It's versatile, too. You can dress it up in individual bowls to serve as a posh starter with toasted sourdough, or you can just whack it in the middle of the table with a pile of raw vegetables and everyone can dip away.

A Cornish style of smoked brandade

Serves 8 as a starter

500g finest smoked haddock
  or smoked pollack, skinned
  and pin-boned
2 large baking potatoes,
  peeled
A pinch of saffron strands
300ml whole milk
2 garlic cloves, peeled and
  finely chopped
2 bay leaves
200ml cold-pressed rapeseed
  oil (ideally Cornish), plus
  a drizzle to finish
2 tbsp flat-leaf parsley leaves,
  finely sliced
Juice of 1 lemon, or to taste
Sea salt and freshly ground
  black pepper

To serve

Sourdough bread, thickly
  sliced

Cut the potatoes into large even-sized chunks and place in a saucepan. Cover with water and add salt and the saffron. Bring to a simmer and cook for about 15 minutes until soft.

Meanwhile, pour the milk into another pan and add the garlic and bay leaves. Bring to a simmer over a medium heat, then add the fish. Take the pan off the heat and leave the fish to cook in the residual heat of the milk for 6 minutes. Remove the fish and flake into a food processor; reserve the milk.

Tip the potatoes into a colander and leave them to drain and dry off for a few minutes. Meanwhile, gently warm the rapeseed oil in a pan.

Purée the fish in the processor then, with the motor running, slowly pour in the warm oil and the reserved milk through the funnel. Once it is all incorporated, add most of the parsley, saving a little for the garnish.

Add the potatoes to the mixture and blitz for 30 seconds. Finally, add most of the lemon juice and a good sprinkling of pepper.

Scrape the brandade into a bowl and give it a good stir. Taste and adjust the seasoning, adding more lemon juice if required.

Just before serving, toast the sourdough slices. Serve the brandade topped with a drizzle of rapeseed oil and the remaining parsley, with the toasted sourdough on the side.

Salmon and whisky is a pairing I've been serving in various ways since I opened my first restaurant, Black Pig, in 2003. Good quality hot-smoked salmon is available from good delis, supermarkets and online – it's well worth buying superior smoked fish because the texture and flavour will be better. If whisky isn't your thing, you could use the same recipe to create a beetroot jelly, swapping the whisky for beetroot juice.

Hot-smoked salmon pâté, whisky jelly

Serves 6 as a starter

For the pâté
400g hot-smoked salmon, skinned
Finely grated zest and juice of 1 lime
100g full-fat cream cheese
150g full-fat Greek yoghurt
1 tbsp creamed horseradish
Sea salt and freshly ground black pepper

For the whisky jelly
2 sheets of bronze leaf gelatine
200ml 'peaty' whisky
40g caster sugar

To serve
12 slices of rye bread
Grated zest of 1 lime

To make the pâté, put the hot-smoked salmon into a food processor with the lime juice and blitz for 20 seconds. Scrape down the sides of the bowl and add the cream cheese, yoghurt, horseradish, lime zest and some salt and pepper. Blitz for 1 minute: you want the pâté to be almost smooth, with a little texture from the salmon. Divide between 6 ramekins or other small dishes, cover and refrigerate.

To make the jelly, soak the gelatine in a shallow dish of ice-cold water for about 5 minutes to soften. Put the whisky and sugar into a pan and heat gently until the sugar has dissolved and the liquor is almost at a simmer.

Remove the gelatine leaves from the dish and squeeze out the excess water. Add to the whisky, off the heat, and stir until melted. Leave to cool completely, but don't let it set.

Pour the cooled, liquid jelly evenly on top of the pâté and return to the fridge to set.

Take the pâté out of the fridge around 20 minutes before serving so that it comes to room temperature.

When ready to eat, toast the rye bread. Sprinkle the lime zest over the pâté and serve immediately, with the toast.

My son Jacob adores this dip. It was originally created as a bar snack to serve with drinks at Outlaw's Fish Kitchen in Port Isaac and has been on the menu ever since. Easy to make, it's a great dish for a party and keeps well in the fridge for 3–4 days. I serve it topped generously with smoked paprika and garlicky olive oil, with a pile of warm flatbreads to tear and scoop up the dip. You should be able to get good smoked cod's roe from your fishmonger, although you may need to order it in advance. Alternatively, you can order it from a reputable online fishmonger.

Jacob's favourite cod's roe dip

Serves 6 as a starter, or up to 10 as a bite

400g smoked cod's roe, rinsed and membrane removed
4 garlic cloves (unpeeled)
500ml olive oil
100g good quality crustless white bread
About 100ml milk
40g Dijon mustard
Juice of 2 lemons
Sea salt and freshly ground black pepper
Smoked paprika to sprinkle

To serve
Flatbreads

Put the garlic and olive oil into a saucepan over a medium heat and heat until the oil starts to bubble around the garlic cloves. Turn the heat down slightly, so that the garlic doesn't fry, and cook gently for 20 minutes. When the garlic is soft, take the pan off the heat. Leave to infuse and cool completely.

Meanwhile, break the bread into chunks and place in a bowl. Pour on the milk and set aside to soak.

When the oil is cold, remove the garlic cloves with a slotted spoon and peel them; reserve the oil.

Put the cod's roe, mustard, lemon juice and garlic into a blender or food processor. Squeeze the bread to remove excess milk, then add to the blender and blitz for 1 minute. With the motor running, slowly add most of the garlic oil through the funnel until the mixture thickens and has the consistency of mayonnaise; save some oil for serving.

Season with salt and pepper to taste and blend for another 20 seconds. Scrape into a bowl, cover and refrigerate until needed.

When ready to serve, sprinkle the dip generously with smoked paprika and drizzle with the reserved garlicky olive oil. Accompany with plenty of warm flatbreads.

I particularly like to cook with Mexican flavours in the summer – it just feels right – and this is a great dish to make when tomatoes are at their peak. Gurnard has a lovely sweet flavour and nice firm texture, which is well suited to deep-frying in this way. Grey mullet and bass also work well here.

Polenta coated gurnard, sweetcorn, red onion and tomato relish, jalapeño mayonnaise

Serves 4 as a starter

2 gurnard, about 600g each,
  filleted and pin-boned
100g plain flour, for coating
2 medium eggs, beaten
150g fine polenta
Sunflower oil for deep-frying
Sea salt and freshly ground
  black pepper

**For the sweetcorn, red onion
and tomato relish**

6 ripe plum tomatoes
2 corn on the cobs
3 tbsp olive oil
4 small red onions, peeled
  and cut into 5mm dice
2 green chillies, deseeded and
  finely chopped
Juice of 2 limes
2 tbsp caster sugar
3 tbsp chopped coriander,
  plus a few sprigs to garnish

For the jalapeño mayonnaise

2 egg yolks
15ml verjus or white wine
  vinegar
30g jalapeño chillies in
  vinegar, drained
250ml sunflower oil
15g flat-leaf parsley, leaves
  picked and chopped
10g coriander, leaves picked
  and chopped
25g rocket leaves, chopped
15g Parmesan, freshly grated

To serve

2 limes, halved

To make the relish, using a small, sharp knife, scoop out the core from each tomato and score a crisscross on the bottom of each one. Place in a bowl, pour on boiling water to cover and leave for 30 seconds. Lift out the tomatoes, peel away the skins and roughly chop the flesh; set aside.

Cut the sweetcorn kernels from the cobs, by standing the cobs upright on a board and cutting downwards with a sharp knife.

Heat a large frying pan over a high heat and add the olive oil. When hot, add the onions, chillies and sweetcorn. Cook, stirring, over a high heat for about 3 minutes until the onions and sweetcorn start to soften and colour. Add the chopped tomatoes with a good pinch of salt and cook for 2 minutes. Remove from the heat and add the lime juice, sugar and coriander. Stir well, then set aside in the pan.

For the mayonnaise, put the egg yolks, verjus and chillies in a blender or small food processor and blitz for 30 seconds. Scrape down the sides of the bowl and blitz again for a few seconds. With the motor running, slowly add half the oil in a thin, steady stream through the funnel. Add the parsley, coriander, rocket, Parmesan and a large pinch of salt. Blend for 1 minute. Add the remaining oil in a steady stream, blending until the mayonnaise is thick. Taste and correct the seasoning, then spoon into a bowl, cover and refrigerate until needed.

Set up three bowls: one with flour, one with beaten eggs and one with polenta. Pass the gurnard fillets through the flour, then the egg and finally the polenta to coat. Place the coated fillets on a plate.

Heat the oil in a deep-fat fryer or other suitable deep, heavy pan to 180°C. Deep-fry the fillets in the hot oil, in batches, for about 3 minutes until golden. Remove and drain on kitchen paper, then sprinkle with salt.

To serve, share the relish between 4 plates. Add a gurnard fillet and a good spoonful of mayonnaise to each plate and finish with a sprig of coriander and a lime half.

Starters and small bites

If any of your friends or family say they don't like oysters, get them to try these. I've converted no end of staunch avoiders with crispy deep-fried oysters! I wouldn't fry – or even cook – a native oyster; it's the cheaper and bigger farmed oysters that you want here. Opening oysters might seem a bit daunting at first but, once you have done a few, you'll become more confident.

Fried oyster bap, cucumber and mint relish

Serves 4 as a snack

12 live rock oysters
100g plain flour, for coating
2 medium eggs, beaten
100g Japanese panko
  breadcrumbs
Sunflower oil for deep-frying
Sea salt and freshly ground
  black pepper

For the cucumber and
  mint relish

2 cucumbers
100ml cider vinegar
50g caster sugar
1 red onion, peeled and finely
  sliced
1 garlic clove, peeled and
  finely chopped
1 tsp fennel seeds
1 green chilli, deseeded and
  finely chopped
2 tbsp chopped mint
1 tbsp chopped flat parsley

To serve

4 floured baps, split almost
  in half
1 bunch of watercress, leaves
  picked

First make the relish. Halve the cucumbers lengthways, then scoop out the seeds with a teaspoon and discard. Slice the cucumber flesh into half-moon shapes and place in a bowl. Season with salt, then leave to draw out the excess water for 30 minutes.

Heat the cider vinegar, sugar, red onion, garlic and fennel seeds in a pan until the sugar has dissolved, then remove from the heat.

Squeeze the cucumber to remove excess water, add to the vinegar mixture and give it a good stir. Leave to cool completely, then stir in the chopped chilli and herbs. Set aside until ready to serve.

Set up three bowls: one with flour, one with beaten eggs and one with breadcrumbs. Open the oysters, drain off the juices and check for any fragments of shell. Pass the oysters through the flour, patting off any excess, then through the egg and finally into the breadcrumbs to coat. The oysters can stay in the breadcrumbs until you are ready to fry them.

When ready to serve, heat the oil in a deep-fat fryer or other suitable deep, heavy pan to 180°C.

Toast your baps and place 2 tbsp of the relish and some watercress on each base.

Deep-fry the oysters in the hot oil for 1 minute until golden and crisp. Remove and drain on kitchen paper. Place 3 crispy oysters on each bap base and close the lid. Serve at once.

This is my version of the Sicilian classic *arancini*. It's a great recipe and a real crowd pleaser. At my first restaurant, I cooked a lobster risotto flavoured with orange, basil and spring onions, which became a signature dish. I've used the same combination here because it works so well.

Lobster risotto balls, basil and orange mayonnaise

Makes about 20; serves 10 as a starter

2 live lobsters, about 800g each
1 litre vegetable stock (see page 218)
250g carnaroli rice
1 bunch of spring onions, trimmed and finely sliced
100g Parmesan, freshly grated
Finely grated zest of 1 orange
30 basil leaves, finely sliced
1 medium egg, beaten
150g plain flour
500g dried breadcrumbs
Sunflower oil for deep-frying
Sea salt and freshly ground black pepper

For the basil and orange mayonnaise

2 egg yolks
Finely grated zest of 1 orange
30ml white wine vinegar
450ml light olive oil
4 spring onions, trimmed and sliced
20 basil leaves, finely sliced

Put the lobsters in the freezer 30 minutes before cooking to sedate them.

Bring a large pan of well salted water to the boil. To kill the lobsters instantly, place them on a board and insert the tip of a strong, sharp knife firmly into the cross on the back of the head, then plunge the lobsters into the boiling water. Bring back to the boil and cook for 8 minutes.

Remove the lobsters from the pan to a tray and leave until cool enough to handle. Twist and pull the claws, legs and head away from the tails. Put the heads into a pan with the vegetable stock. Crack the claws and extract the meat. Using scissors, cut open the tail shell along its length. Pull the shell apart and remove the tail meat in one piece. Cut this meat in half lengthways and remove the dark intestinal tract. Cut the tail and claw meat into small pieces, put into a bowl, cover and refrigerate.

For the lobster balls, bring the stock (and lobster heads) to the boil. Add the rice with a pinch of salt and bring back to the boil. Lower the heat and simmer until the rice has absorbed all the stock. Take off the heat and discard the heads. Stir in the spring onions, Parmesan, orange zest and some pepper. Spread the rice out on a tray and cool in the fridge.

Meanwhile, for the mayonnaise, put the egg yolks, orange zest and wine vinegar into a blender or small food processor and blend for 30 seconds then, with the motor running, slowly add the olive oil in a steady stream. If it gets too thick, add 1 tsp water, then continue. Transfer to a bowl, stir in the spring onions, basil and salt and pepper to taste; set aside.

Once the rice is cold, stir in the sliced basil and lobster meat. Break off pieces and roll into balls, roughly the size of a golf ball. In a bowl, mix the beaten egg and flour together with some salt and pepper until smoothly combined. Place the breadcrumbs on a tray. Heat the oil in a deep-fat fryer or other suitable deep, heavy pan to 160°C.

Pass the lobster balls through the egg mix and then into the breadcrumbs, turning to coat all over. Deep-fry in the hot oil, in batches if necessary, for about 2 minutes until crisp and golden. Drain on kitchen paper and season with salt. Serve hot or cold, with the mayonnaise on the side.

Starters and small bites

This is a breakfast treat for all seafood lovers. Bottarga – the salted, pressed, air-dried roe of either tuna or grey mullet – is considered to be one of the great food delicacies of the world. Of the two, I prefer the more refined, subtle flavour of grey mullet bottarga, which is also more sustainable. The keta caviar – salmon roe – is a lovely addition. To give the dish a comforting feel, I sit the poached eggs on a creamy horseradish mash and liven it up with a grating of fresh horseradish at the end.

Poached eggs with bottarga, salmon roe and horseradish mash

Serves 4

1 bottarga, about 100g (you won't need all of it for this recipe)
100g keta caviar (ideally wild Alaskan)
8 large eggs
50ml white wine vinegar

For the horseradish mash
3 large baking potatoes
1 fresh horseradish root, peeled
150ml single cream
100ml whole milk
Sea salt and freshly ground black pepper

To serve
1 lemon, cut into 4 wedges

Preheat your oven to 200°C/Fan 185°C/Gas 6.

For the mash, bake the potatoes on an oven tray for 1 hour or until tender. Set aside until cool enough to handle. Meanwhile, grate 50g of the horseradish and put into a saucepan with the cream and milk. Bring to a simmer and remove from the heat.

Cut the potatoes in half, scoop out the flesh and pass through a potato ricer into a bowl, or mash with a potato masher. Fold in the creamy milk to give a soft mash texture. Season with salt and pepper to taste, bearing in mind the bottarga and keta are salty. Keep warm.

To poach the eggs, bring a large pan of water to a simmer with the wine vinegar added. Crack each egg into a small individual cup or ramekin and add to the simmering water. (There is no need to stir the water – if your eggs are fresh they will form a nice shape instantly.) Cook the eggs for 3 minutes.

Meanwhile, lay some kitchen paper on a plate ready to drain the eggs. When the eggs are cooked, remove them with a slotted spoon and trim away the escaping bits of egg white if you wish. Drain on the kitchen paper and season with salt and pepper.

Spoon a portion of horseradish mash onto each of 4 warmed plates and make a well in the middle with the back of the spoon. Place 2 poached eggs in each well and slice the bottarga over the top. Add small spoonfuls of keta, followed by a good grating of horseradish. Serve immediately, with a wedge of lemon.

Believe it or not, this is where it all started for me, with those bright orange crumbed fish bricks from the magic cold place! I'd like to tell you that my love of fish started with bouillabaisse in Provence, or whole turbot cooked over coals in San Sebastian, but no, it was the humble fish finger. Now, of course, I make my own. Eaten burger-style, with lettuce, gherkins and a pea and mint mayonnaise, they are surprisingly good. For a buffet or kids' party, buy smaller rolls and cut smaller fish fingers.

Fish finger roll, pea and mint mayonnaise

Serves 4 as a snack

600g haddock fillet, skinned,
  pin-boned and cut into
  fingers
100g plain flour, for coating
2 medium eggs, beaten
100g breadcrumbs
Sunflower oil for deep-frying
Sea salt and freshly ground
  black pepper

**For the pea and mint
  mayonnaise**
2 egg yolks
100g fresh or frozen peas
1 tsp English mustard
5 tsp malt vinegar
2 tbsp chopped mint
300ml sunflower oil

To serve
1 iceberg lettuce, finely
  shredded
2 large gherkins, grated
4 good quality focaccia or
  other large rolls, split in half
1 lemon, cut into wedges

First make the mayonnaise. Put the egg yolks, peas, mustard, vinegar and half of the mint into a blender or small food processor and blend for 30 seconds. Then, with the motor running, add the oil in a slow, steady stream through the funnel until it is fully emulsified. Stop the machine and add the remaining mint and some salt and pepper, then blend for 30 seconds. Transfer the mayonnaise to a tub, check the seasoning and refrigerate until needed.

Set up three bowls: one with the flour, one with beaten eggs and one with breadcrumbs. Pass the fish, one piece at a time, though the flour and pat off any excess, then through the egg, and finally through the breadcrumbs. Place the breaded fish on a plate. Heat the oil in a deep-fat fryer or other suitable deep, heavy pan to 180°C.

Combine the shredded lettuce and grated gherkins with 2 tbsp of the mayonnaise and mix well, then share equally between the roll bases.

Now fry your fish fingers for 4 minutes until golden and crisp, turning as necessary to colour evenly. When the fish is ready, drain on a plate lined with kitchen paper and season well with salt.

Lay the hot fish fingers on the rolls and top with a dollop of mayonnaise. Close the lids and serve immediately, with lemon wedges.

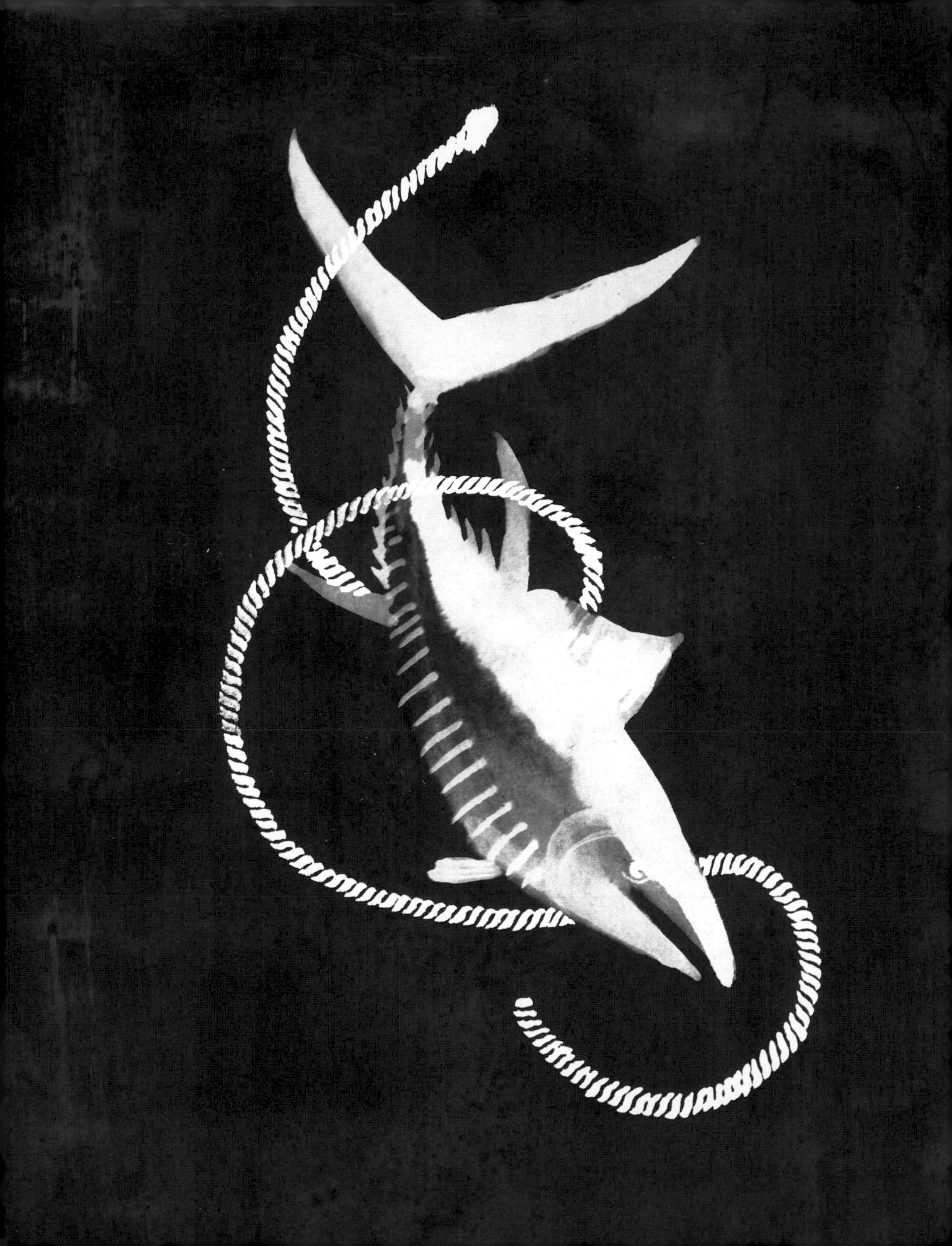

STRAIGHT

FROM

THE SEA

Raw scallops always go down well when we serve them in the restaurants so I wanted to share a favourite recipe of mine here. Prepare it during the autumn and winter, when celeriac is at its best. I make a stock and a pickle from the celeriac and finish the dish with celeriac crisps and a drizzle of chilli oil.

Raw scallops, celeriac broth and green chilli

Serves 4 as a starter

12 very fresh scallops, shelled, cleaned and roes removed

For the celeriac broth

1 large or 2 small celeriac, peeled and diced
2 tbsp sunflower oil
A good squeeze of lemon juice
Sea salt

For the celeriac pickle

½ celeriac, peeled and cut into matchsticks
75ml cider
75ml cider vinegar
75ml water
75g caster sugar
A small handful of coriander, leaves picked and chopped

For the celeriac crisps

½ celeriac, peeled
Sunflower oil for deep-frying

For the green chilli oil

30g coriander, leaves picked
300ml light olive oil
2 green chillies, chopped (seeds left in)

To finish

1–2 green chilli(es), deseeded and finely chopped

First make the chilli oil. Add the coriander to a pan of boiling salted water and blanch for 30 seconds, then lift out and plunge into a bowl of cold water to refresh. Drain and squeeze out the excess water, then place in a blender. Add the olive oil and chillies and blitz thoroughly. Pour into a container and place in the fridge for 24 hours. Decant just before serving.

For the broth, weigh the diced celeriac and note the weight. Heat a pan (large enough to hold the celeriac comfortably) and add the olive oil. Add the celeriac and cook over a medium heat until caramelised all over, at least 20 minutes. Add the same volume of water as the weight of the celeriac and bring to the boil. Lower the heat and simmer for 20 minutes.

Strain the liquid into a clean pan. (Save the celeriac for a stew or mash with your next meal.) Bring the liquor to a simmer and let bubble until reduced to about 150ml; it should be a lovely golden brown colour. Strain again and allow to cool. Cover and refrigerate until required.

For the pickle, put the celeriac matchsticks into a bowl. Heat the cider, vinegar, water, sugar and a pinch of salt in a small pan to dissolve the sugar and bring to the boil. Pour over the celeriac, cover and let cool.

For the crisps, finely slice the celeriac, using a mandoline, if you have one. Heat the oil in a deep-fat fryer or other suitable deep, heavy pan to 150°C. Line a tray with kitchen paper. Fry the celeriac slices in batches, as necessary: lower into the hot oil and fry until golden all over. Remove with a strainer, drain on the kitchen paper and sprinkle with sea salt. Allow to cool.

To assemble, drain the pickled celeriac and toss the chopped coriander through it. On a clean board with a sharp knife, slice the scallops in half horizontally and season with a little salt.

Share the scallops and celeriac between 4 warmed shallow bowls. Gently warm the broth in a pan and add salt and lemon juice to taste. Divide equally between the bowls and finish with a drizzle of chilli oil and a sprinkling of chillies. Serve at once, garnished with the celeriac crisps.

This dish is really quick and fun to make. You can even let your guests do it for themselves if you want! The most important thing is to get hold of some super-fresh salmon. I use good-quality, organically farmed salmon; for me it works perfectly in the raw and cured salmon dishes I serve.

Raw salmon with vodka, orange and horseradish

Serves 4 as a starter

400g very fresh salmon fillet, skinned
1 orange
1 bunch of spring onions, trimmed and finely sliced on the diagonal
2 tbsp freshly grated horseradish
6–8 tbsp lemon vodka
8 tbsp olive oil
Sea salt
Tarragon leaves, to finish

Chill 4 flat serving plates in the fridge. Cut away the peel and pith from the orange, then cut out the segments from between the membranes. Cut the orange flesh into small pieces.

Using a very sharp knife and a clean board, slice the salmon thinly (or dice it into small pieces if you find it easier).

Lay the slices of salmon on the chilled plates. Sprinkle with a little salt, then scatter over the spring onions, orange and horseradish.

Mix together the vodka and olive oil and spoon over the salmon equally. Garnish with tarragon leaves and eat immediately.

Tuna served this way is just fantastic. Taking a beautiful loin of tuna and searing it very quickly in a hot pan does so much for the flavour, because the inside stays raw and contrasts beautifully with the seared exterior. The sauce is based on a classic salsa verde, with the addition of green olives. It's a great dish for a party because it can be prepared in advance.

Raw tuna with green olive sauce

Serves 4 as a starter

600g very fresh loin of tuna
  (yellowfin)
Light olive oil for cooking
Sea salt and freshly ground
  black pepper

For the green olive sauce
3 spring onions, trimmed and
  thinly sliced
1 garlic clove, peeled and
  finely grated
2 tbsp capers in wine vinegar,
  drained
4 tbsp pitted green olives
4 good quality tinned anchovy
  fillets in oil, drained
Finely grated zest and juice
  of 1 lemon
A handful of flat-leaf parsley,
  leaves picked
½ handful of mint, leaves
  picked
100ml olive oil
20 basil leaves, finely sliced

Season the tuna loin all over with salt and pepper. Have ready a bowl of iced water big enough to hold the tuna loin.

Place a non-stick heavy-based frying pan over a high heat until the pan is very hot. Lightly oil the tuna and lay it in the hot pan. Sear evenly all over, turning as necessary, then plunge the tuna into the iced water to stop the cooking. Once it is cool, lift out and pat dry with kitchen paper. Place the tuna in a suitable plastic container and chill in the fridge for at least 30 minutes until ready to serve.

To make the sauce, put the spring onions, garlic, capers, olives and anchovies on a board, sprinkle with the lemon zest and chop together until the mixture almost turns into a paste. Transfer to a bowl.

Chop the parsley and mint leaves together, add to the sauce and mix well. Add the lemon juice and olive oil and mix again. Season with salt and pepper to taste. Finally add the sliced basil and fork through. Set aside to allow the flavours to mingle (but not in the fridge).

I like to slice the tuna and lay it out on one large plate to place in the centre of the table, but you can plate it individually if you wish. Sprinkle with a little sea salt and serve with the green olive sauce.

Like turbot, brill has a lovely firm texture that makes it ideal for curing and easier to slice once cured than other flat fish varieties. It just takes the salt a bit longer to work its magic though the dense flesh. This is my version of a dish that Pete Biggs, my longstanding head chef, developed. The balance between all the components is lovely. Turbot works equally well here, or try very fresh plaice instead – reducing the curing time by an hour.

Citrus-cured brill with anchovy mayonnaise, basil and pistachios

Serves 4 as a starter

500g very fresh brill fillets, skinned and trimmed

For the cure
100g sea salt
80g caster sugar
Grated zest of 1 lemon
Grated zest of 1 lime
Grated zest of 1 orange
100ml white wine

For the anchovy mayonnaise
2 egg yolks
1 tsp English mustard
4 good quality tinned anchovy fillets in oil, drained
3 tbsp water
2 tbsp lemon juice
300ml sunflower oil
Sea salt and freshly ground black pepper

To finish
4 tbsp pistachio nuts roasted in the shell, shelled and roughly chopped if preferred
8 basil leaves, thinly sliced
Basil oil (see page 216) or olive oil to drizzle

For the cure, put the sea salt, sugar, citrus zests and white wine into a food processor and blitz for 1 minute. Lay the brill fillets on a tray and sprinkle the mixture over them. Turn the fillets over in the cure a few times to ensure they are coated all over. Put into a suitable plastic container and place in the fridge to cure for 3 hours.

To make the mayonnaise, put the egg yolks, mustard, anchovies, water and lemon juice into a small food processor and blitz for 1 minute. With the motor running, slowly add the oil in a thin, steady stream through the funnel until it is all incorporated. Season with salt and pepper to taste. Transfer to a bowl, cover and refrigerate until needed.

When the time is up, wash the cure off the brill fillets with cold water and pat dry with kitchen paper. Lay the fish in a suitable plastic container and place back in the fridge for an hour to firm up. (At this stage you can freeze the fish for up to 1 month.)

Using a sharp knife and a clean board, slice the brill thinly and lay it equally on 4 plates. Spoon on the mayonnaise, in small blobs, so you have some with each mouthful of fish.

Finish with a sprinkling of chopped pistachios and sliced basil. Finally, drizzle on some basil or olive oil. Serve cold or at room temperature.

Verjus is a natural grape product that we use in various ways in our kitchens. It isn't something you would usually associate with curing fish but I was determined to give it a try and after a few attempts I came up with this recipe. I think the simplicity of this dish is beautiful. The textures of the pumpkin seeds and grapes work so well with the soft cured monkfish.

Verjus-cured monkfish with pumpkin seeds and grape dressing

Serves 4 as a starter
600g very fresh monkfish
   fillet, skinned and trimmed

For the cure
200g sea salt
100g caster sugar
2 tbsp rosemary leaves
100ml verjus

For the grape dressing
2 shallots, peeled and finely
   chopped
100ml verjus
2 tsp Dijon mustard
100ml olive oil
10 green seedless grapes,
   sliced
10 red seedless grapes, sliced
Sea salt

For the garnish
400ml sunflower oil, for
   deep-frying
150g pumpkin seeds
Finely grated zest of 1 lemon
2 tsp finely sliced flat-leaf
   parsley leaves

For the cure, put the salt, sugar and rosemary into a food processor and blitz thoroughly.

Lay the monkfish in the bottom of a plastic container big enough to hold it in one layer. Sprinkle evenly with the salt mixture, turning the fish over a few times to ensure it is coated all over. Drizzle the verjus evenly over the fish, then put the lid on and place in the fridge for 3 hours to cure.

When the time is up, take the fish out of the container and wash off the cure with cold water, then pat dry with kitchen paper. Put the fish back into a clean container and place back in the fridge for an hour to firm up. (At this point you can freeze the fish for up to a month.)

To prepare the pumpkin seed garnish, put the oil in a small, deep, heavy pan, add the pumpkin seeds and heat slowly over a medium heat until the seeds begin to puff up. As soon as they start to pop, carefully take the pan off the heat. Using a slotted spoon, remove the seeds from the oil and drain them on a tray lined with kitchen paper. Season with salt and allow to cool.

To make the dressing, put the shallots and verjus into a small pan, bring to the boil and then tip the contents of the pan into a bowl. Add the mustard and whisk to combine. Now add the olive oil in a slow, steady stream, whisking all the time. Season with salt to taste and add the sliced grapes.

Using a sharp knife and a clean board, slice the monkfish as thinly as possible and lay it equally on 4 large plates. Spoon the dressing over the fish, sharing the grapes evenly. Scatter over the lemon zest, parsley and pumpkin seeds, then serve.

Wild sea trout is, for me, a delicacy. I actually prefer it to salmon and find it responds particularly well to curing. Using strong alcohol in the cure helps to achieve a pronounced flavour and the combination of gin, apple and fennel works well here. This is a good dish for a party because it can be prepared in advance and whipped out of the fridge when you're ready to serve.

Gin-cured sea trout with apple and fennel

Serves 6 as a starter

1 very fresh side of wild
  sea trout, skinned and
  pin-boned

For the cure

250g sea salt
250g caster sugar
2 tbsp juniper berries, crushed
150ml gin

**For the apple and fennel
  salad**

200ml olive oil
2 shallots, peeled and finely
  sliced
4 juniper berries, finely
  chopped
100ml cider vinegar
30ml gin
2 fennel bulbs, tough outer
  layer removed
3 eating apples, such as
  Braeburn
3 tsp finely sliced tarragon

For the cure, put the salt, sugar and crushed juniper berries into a food processor and blitz for 3 minutes.

Lay the sea trout on a suitable lidded plastic tray and sprinkle evenly with the cure mixture. Turn the fish over in the cure a few times to make sure it is coated all over. Drizzle the gin evenly over the fish, then pop the lid on and place in the fridge to cure for 4 hours.

When the time is up, take the fish out of the tray and wash off the cure with cold water, then pat dry with kitchen paper. Put the fish back into a clean container and place back in the fridge for an hour to firm up. (At this point you can freeze the fish for up to a month.)

To make the dressing, put the olive oil, shallots and chopped juniper berries into a small pan over a medium heat until the oil just begins to bubble. Take the pan off the heat and add the cider vinegar and gin.

Slice the fennel as thinly as possible, using a mandoline if you have one, and place it in a bowl. Peel, core and grate the apples, then add to the fennel with the tarragon. Toss to combine and dress the salad with half of the dressing, keeping the rest to finish the dish.

Using a sharp knife and a clean board, slice the trout as thinly as possible and lay it equally on 4 large plates. Scatter some of the salad over the fish and drizzle with the remaining dressing; bring to room temperature before serving. Serve the rest of the salad in a bowl on the side.

Eating mackerel raw, straight out of the sea, is something everyone should try. The texture and flavour is unique, indeed I would go so far as saying that flavourwise mackerel is the best fish to eat raw. Marrying it with apple, celery and bacon is really successful. This same dish works well with salmon, trout or scallops.

Raw mackerel with apple, celery and bacon

Serves 4 as a starter

2 very fresh large mackerel, filleted, pin-boned and skinned
4 rashers of smoked streaky bacon
I eating apple, such as Braeburn
I shallot, peeled and finely chopped
2 tsp chopped chervil
2 tsp chopped chives
3 tbsp mayonnaise (see page 219)
Sea salt and freshly ground black pepper

For the pickled celery

3 celery sticks, de-stringed (with a peeler)
75ml white wine
75ml white wine vinegar
75ml water
75g caster sugar
I tsp fennel seeds

To assemble and serve

4 slices of wholemeal or seeded bread, for toasting
A handful of watercress, stalks removed
Cold-pressed rapeseed oil to drizzle
Lemon wedges

First, prepare the pickled celery. Finely slice the celery and set aside. Heat the wine, wine vinegar, water, sugar and fennel seeds in a pan to dissolve the sugar. Add a pinch of salt and bring to the boil. Take the pan off the heat and add the celery. Cover with a disc of greaseproof paper, pushing it down onto the surface to keep the celery fully submerged in the liquor. Leave to cool.

Preheat your grill to the highest setting. Lay the bacon on the grill rack and grill on both sides until crispy. When cool enough to handle, chop the bacon and set aside.

Using a very sharp knife and a clean board, slice the mackerel into 5mm thick slices. Peel, quarter and core the apple, then cut into small dice.

Put the mackerel and diced apple into a bowl with the shallot, bacon and herbs. Toss everything together well and add the mayonnaise. Mix well again and taste for seasoning – a grinding of pepper will probably be welcome, but the bacon may well provide enough salt.

To serve, drain the pickled celery. Toast the bread on both sides and place on the serving plates. Share the mackerel mixture equally between the slices of toast. Scatter the watercress over the plates and put a pile of pickled celery on one side.

Finish with a drizzle of rapeseed oil and serve with lemon wedges.

This is a great spring/summer dish. The fish takes on all of the curry flavour and its texture is transformed. Pickled peppers, coconut yoghurt and fragrant coriander balance it perfectly. This dish will also work well with bass, bream and mackerel.

Curry-cured grey mullet with pickled peppers and coconut yoghurt

Serves 4 as a starter
500g very fresh grey mullet
   fillet, skinned and pin-boned

For the cure
50g fine sea salt
50g caster sugar
20g hot curry powder

For the pickled peppers
1 red pepper
1 yellow pepper
75ml white wine
75ml white wine vinegar
75ml water
75g caster sugar
1 garlic clove, peeled and
   crushed

For the coconut yoghurt
200g full-fat Greek yoghurt
100g thick coconut milk
Sea salt

To finish
2 tsp chopped coriander
Curry oil (see page 216)
   to drizzle
Micro coriander cress
   (optional)

For the cure, mix the salt, sugar and curry powder together in a bowl. Lay the fish on a suitable lidded plastic tray and sprinkle evenly with the cure mixture. Turn the fish over in the cure a few times to ensure it is coated all over. Put the lid on and place in the fridge to cure for 6 hours.

For the pickled peppers, peel, halve, core and deseed the peppers. Slice the peppers thinly and place in a bowl. Put the wine, wine vinegar, water and sugar into a small pan and heat to dissolve the sugar, then bring to the boil. Add the crushed garlic clove and pour the over peppers. Cover the bowl with a disc of greaseproof paper and leave to cool.

For the coconut yoghurt, mix the yoghurt and coconut milk together in a bowl until evenly combined and season with salt to taste. Cover and refrigerate until ready to serve.

When the curing time is up, wash the cure off the fish in cold water and pat dry with kitchen paper. Put the fish in a suitable plastic container with a lid and return to the fridge for an hour to firm up.

Slice the grey mullet as thinly as possible and share between 4 plates. Drain the peppers and toss them with the coriander and a drizzle of curry oil. Taste for seasoning, adding a little salt if you like.

Share the peppers between the 4 plates, finishing with spoonfuls of the yoghurt, extra curry oil and coriander cress, if using.

Salmon has the perfect texture and balance of oiliness for curing. I like to experiment with different cures and this combination of beer and seaweed is something I came up with for a charity dinner. It's always a challenge to cook fish for large numbers, so I decided not to cook it at all, but cure it instead! Fortunately it went down well. The cucumber and seaweed salad is the ideal complement.

Beer-cured salmon with cucumber and seaweed salad

Serves 4

500g very fresh wild or
  organic farmed salmon,
  trimmed and skinned

For the cure
100g sea salt
100g soft brown sugar
150ml strong beer

For the cucumber and
  seaweed salad
1 large cucumber
100ml olive oil
70ml light rapeseed oil
50ml white wine vinegar
1 large shallot, peeled and
  finely chopped
2 tsp mixed seaweed flakes
Sea salt

For the salad cream
2 egg yolks
2 tsp dried seaweed
2 tsp English mustard
2 tsp caster sugar
2 tbsp lemon juice
100ml rapeseed oil
150ml double cream

To garnish
1 tbsp dried seaweed flakes

To cure the salmon, lay the fish in a suitable lidded plastic container and sprinkle evenly with the salt and sugar. Turn the fish over in the cure a few times to ensure it is coated all over. Drizzle evenly with the beer, then put the lid on and place in the fridge to cure for 6 hours.

For the cucumber salad, put the oils and wine vinegar into a pan with the shallot, seaweed and a pinch of salt. Bring to a simmer over a medium heat and let bubble for 2 minutes, then remove from the heat and allow to cool.

Meanwhile, halve the cucumber lengthways, peel, then scoop out and discard the seeds. Thinly slice the cucumber into half-moon shapes. Lay the cucumber slices in a dish and pour the cooled liquor over them. Cover with a disc of greaseproof paper and weigh it down with a saucer so that it is pushed down on the surface to keep the cucumber fully submerged. Leave to stand for at least an hour.

To make the salad cream, whisk the egg yolks, seaweed, mustard, sugar and lemon juice together in a bowl for 1 minute, then gradually whisk in the rapeseed oil, a little at a time, until fully incorporated. To finish, slowly whisk in the cream and season with salt to taste. Cover and refrigerate until required.

When the salmon curing time is up, take the fish out of the container and wash off the cure under cold running water, then pat dry with kitchen paper. Put the fish back into a clean container with a lid and place back in the fridge for an hour to firm up.

To serve, slice the cured salmon into 1cm thick pieces and divide between 4 plates.

For the dressing, drain off some of the liquor from the cucumber salad into a bowl and add some of the shallots too. Arrange some of the cucumber salad over the salmon and spoon on the dressing. Dress the plates with salad cream and seaweed flakes; bring to room temperature before serving. Serve the rest of the salad in a bowl on the side.

This dish has a real kick to it from the ginger and basil, but the mackerel is well up to handling those bold flavours. It would be perfect for a light lunch, or you could easily scale it up for a dinner party. If you have any chutney left over, keep it in the fridge to serve with cheese, cold meats etc. Salmon is a great alternative to the mackerel; just give it an extra 3 hours' curing.

Ginger-cured mackerel, beetroot chutney

Serves 4

4 large mackerel, heads
  removed, gutted, filleted
  and pin-boned

For the cure
200g sea salt
150g caster sugar
2 tsp black peppercorns
2 tsp coriander seeds
100g fresh ginger, peeled and
  grated

For the beetroot chutney
100ml olive oil
1 red onion, peeled and finely
  chopped
1 garlic clove, peeled and
  finely chopped
50g fresh ginger, grated
600g fresh beetroot, peeled
  and grated
300g brown sugar
600ml cider vinegar
2 bay leaves
4 Granny Smith apples,
  peeled, cored and grated
Sea salt and freshly ground
  black pepper

**For the basil and ginger
  crème fraîche**
75g fresh ginger, peeled and
  grated
20 large basil leaves
200ml full-fat crème fraîche

To finish
Cold-pressed rapeseed oil

For the cure, put the salt, sugar, peppercorns and coriander seeds into a food processor and blitz for 3 minutes. Add the grated ginger and blitz for another 2 minutes.

Lay the mackerel fillets on a plastic lidded tray and sprinkle evenly with the cure mixture. Turn the fillets over in the cure a few times to ensure they are coated all over. Put the lid on the tray and place in the fridge to cure for 1 hour.

Meanwhile, make the chutney. Heat the olive oil in a large pan over a medium heat. When it is hot, add the onion, garlic and ginger. Sweat for 1 minute, then add the beetroot and sweat for a further 2 minutes. Now add the brown sugar and cider vinegar and bring the mixture to a simmer. Add the bay leaves and let simmer until the liquid becomes syrupy. Add the grated apples and cook for 10 minutes, stirring occasionally. Transfer to a bowl, season with salt and pepper to taste and leave to cool.

For the crème fraîche, put the grated ginger and basil leaves into a blender with the crème fraîche. Blitz for 2 minutes until smooth. Season with salt and whiz for another 30 seconds. Transfer to a bowl, cover and refrigerate until ready to serve.

When the fish curing time is up, take the fish from the tray and wash off the cure with cold water, then pat dry with kitchen paper.

Slice the fish as thinly as possible and arrange it on 4 plates. Spoon the beetroot chutney into the centre and finish with a drizzle of rapeseed oil. Serve the basil and ginger crème fraîche on the side.

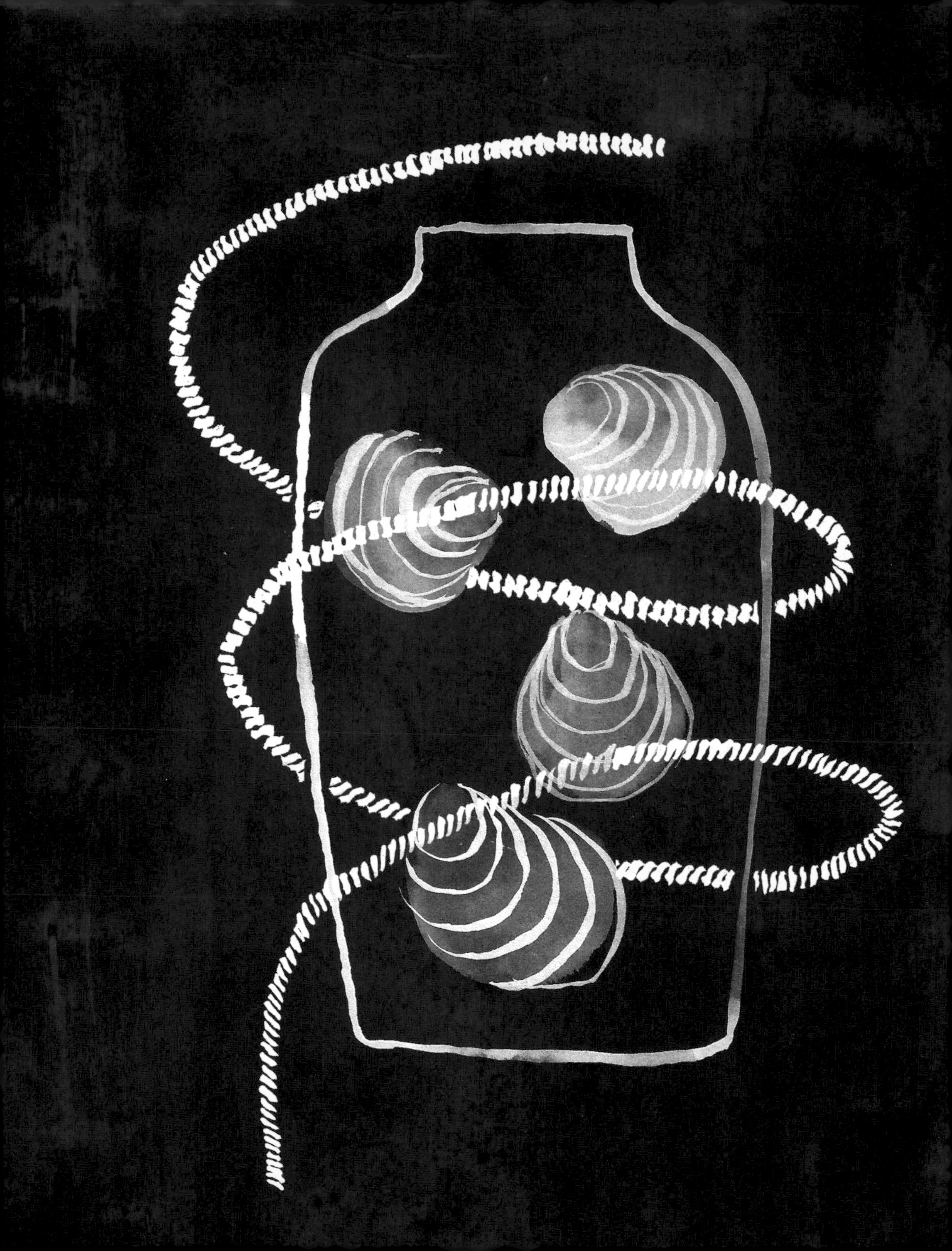

IN A PICKLE

These oysters are a great party snack. You can get everything done beforehand and just dish them up when you are ready. If you're not mad about raw oysters, then try deep-frying them. Coat the oysters in flour, then beaten egg and finally, breadcrumbs. Fry them in hot oil for a few minutes, drain on kitchen paper and serve with the relish on the side.

Cider-pickled oysters with shallot, caper and apple relish

Serves 4 as a starter

12 live Pacific oysters
100ml cider vinegar
100ml olive oil
2 large banana shallots, peeled and finely chopped
1 red chilli, deseeded and finely diced
1 tbsp small capers in brine, drained and rinsed
2 Granny Smith apples
1 tbsp chopped tarragon
1 tbsp chopped dill

To serve
Rock salt or seaweed

Open the oysters and strain their juice through a muslin-lined sieve into a measuring jug. Keep the shells.

Pour 100ml of the oyster juice into a bowl and add the cider vinegar, olive oil, shallots, chilli and capers. Peel and core the apples and cut into fine julienne. Add to the bowl and mix well.

Now add the oysters and mix gently. Cover with a disc of greaseproof paper, pushing it down onto the surface and weighing it down with a small plate if necessary so that all the oysters remain submerged. Leave to pickle for 2 hours.

To serve, clean and dry the oyster shells thoroughly. Place the shells on a bed of seaweed or salt to hold them steady.

Remove the oysters from the bowl and place one in each shell. Stir the chopped herbs through the relish. Top the oysters with a generous spoonful of the relish and serve immediately.

In a pickle

When I opened my Fish Kitchen in Port Isaac, we put this dish on the menu and it went down a storm. The pickled vegetables are a relatively recent addition – I think they bring the whole thing alive.

Beer-marinated seafood

Serves 8 as a starter

1 octopus (double sucker species), about 1kg, defrosted if frozen
1kg live mussels
1kg live cockles
500g raw prawns, heads removed, peeled and deveined
500ml IPA beer
3 bay leaves
4 thyme sprigs
2 garlic cloves, peeled, halved and germ removed
100g marinated anchovy fillets
100ml cold-pressed rapeseed oil
Freshly ground black pepper

For the pickled vegetables
250ml white wine vinegar
250ml water
250g soft brown sugar
2 banana shallots, peeled and sliced
1 fennel bulb, outer layer removed, thinly sliced (ideally on a mandoline)
2 carrots, peeled and sliced into julienne (ideally on a mandoline)
Sea salt

Put the octopus into a pan with the beer, bay, thyme and garlic. Pour on enough water to cover and bring to the boil over a medium heat. Skim off any impurities, lower the heat and simmer for 1 hour until tender.

Meanwhile, prepare the pickled vegetables. Put the wine vinegar, water and sugar into a pan and heat to dissolve the sugar. Bring to a simmer, season with salt and simmer for 2 minutes. Put the shallots, fennel and carrots into a bowl and pour on the hot pickling liquor. Cover with a disc of greaseproof paper, pushing it down onto the surface with a saucer to keep the vegetables submerged.

To cook the mussels and cockles, place a large saucepan (with a tight-fitting lid) over a high heat. When hot, add the mussels, cockles and a ladleful of the octopus stock. Cover and cook for 2 minutes. Check if the shells are open. If not, put the lid back on and continue to cook, checking every 30 seconds until all or most are open.

Tip the contents of the pan into a colander set over a bowl to catch the juices. Discard any unopened molluscs. When cool enough to handle, pick the meat out of the shells. Pour the juices through a muslin-lined sieve into the octopus pan. Refrigerate the mussels and cockles.

Lift the cooked octopus out of the pan; strain and reserve the liquor. Cut the tentacles from the body. Slit open the body and remove the ink sac, stomach and eyes. Slice the tentacles and body meat into 3–4cm pieces.

Strain off the liquor from the veg into a pan and add the same volume of octopus stock. Bring to the boil, skim if necessary, then add the prawns and immediately take off the heat. After 2 minutes, remove the prawns with a slotted spoon; set aside to cool with the octopus. Cool the liquor.

Add the mussels, cockles, octopus, prawns, anchovies and vegetables to the cooled liquor. Mix well, then leave to marinate and pickle overnight.

To serve, drain the seafood and vegetables, reserving the liquor. Season with pepper to taste. Lay on a large platter. Mix 200ml of the pickling liquor with the rapeseed oil and use to dress the salad. Serve with bread.

Every time I buy razor clams I smile as I think of the very first person who ate them – they must have been adventurous and very hungry. If you've ever seen a live razor clam, you will understand what I mean. Thank goodness they are so tasty! Here, I lightly pickle the razors and serve them with a crunchy carrot and fennel chutney and a spicy and cooling yoghurt... delicious.

Razor clams, carrot and fennel chutney, jalapeño yoghurt

Serves 4 as a starter
20 live razor clams
Sea salt

For the pickling liquor
75ml cider vinegar
75ml cider
75ml water
50g caster sugar

For the carrot and fennel chutney
1 fennel bulb, tough outer layer removed
2 carrots, peeled
1 shallot, peeled and finely sliced
1 red chilli, deseeded and finely sliced
50ml cider vinegar
50g caster sugar
1 tsp fennel seeds
1 tsp onion seeds
2 tbsp finely sliced coriander
1 tbsp finely sliced mint, plus extra to finish

For the jalapeño yoghurt
200g full-fat Greek yoghurt
3 tsp chopped jalapeño chillies in vinegar, drained
2 tsp chopped mint

Set up a steamer. Lay the razor clams on a tray and steam for 2 minutes until they open. Carefully remove the razors from the steamer and save their juices. Allow to cool slightly, then remove from their shells. Prepare the razors by cutting away the dark and sandy parts, reserving the white, creamy pieces. Clean the 12 best shells and set aside for use later.

For the pickling liquor, put all the ingredients into a pan and heat to dissolve the sugar, then bring to a simmer and simmer for 2 minutes. Add a pinch of salt, remove from the heat and leave to cool.

When the pickling liquor is cold, add the razor clams, cover and place in the fridge to pickle for at least 30 minutes.

For the chutney, finely slice the fennel, using a mandoline if you have one. Grate the carrots or cut into very fine julienne and place in a bowl with the fennel. Put the shallot and chilli into a small pan with the cider vinegar, sugar, fennel seeds and onion seeds. Heat to dissolve the sugar, then bring to a simmer and pour the mixture over the carrot and fennel. Mix well and season with salt to taste. Finally, stir through the coriander and mint.

For the yoghurt, in a bowl, mix the yoghurt with the chopped jalapeños and mint. Season with salt to taste, then cover and chill until required.

To serve, mix the razor clam meat and chutney together. Spoon into the cleaned shells and place three on each serving plate. Spoon some of the jalapeño yoghurt onto each shell and sprinkle with a little extra mint. Serve straight away.

It doesn't get much simpler than this Peruvian style dish. It's such a great, healthy way to eat seafood and makes a lovely starter for a dinner party. All you need is really fresh fish. Here I've used bass, but I've also made it successfully with salmon, mackerel, brill and scallops. Just be sure to taste it as you go: it's important to get the balance of the heat from the chilli, the acidity from the lime and the level of saltiness right.

A simple bass ceviche

Serves 4 as a starter

400g very fresh bass fillet, skinned, pin-boned and trimmed
1 small red onion, peeled and finely chopped
2 green chillies, deseeded and finely chopped
150g good quality baby plum tomatoes, halved lengthways
Finely grated zest of 1 lime
Juice of 2 limes
A handful of coriander, leaves picked and chopped
2 ripe avocados
Sea salt

To serve

200ml soured cream
Olive oil to drizzle
1 lime, cut into wedges

Cut the bass into dice and place in a bowl with the red onion, chillies, tomatoes, lime zest and juice. Season with salt and add the chopped coriander. Toss well to mix, then cover and leave to cure in the fridge for 10 minutes.

Just before serving, halve, peel and stone the avocados, then cut into dice, the same size as the bass pieces. Toss the avocado through the bass mixture. Taste for seasoning and add more salt if needed.

Divide the ceviche between 4 plates. Top with a dollop of soured cream and add a drizzle of olive oil to each plate. Serve with lime wedges.

Grey mullet is really tasty so it's a shame it has acquired a bad reputation, owing to its liking for brackish and stagnant waters. Your fishmonger should be able to reassure you that his or her fish has been caught in clean water. The oiliness of the flesh partly accounts for its excellent flavour; it also works well in a dish like this. Based on a ceviche, citrus juice cooks the fish and turns it into something fantastic. If you can't get grey mullet, use bass or bream instead.

Grey mullet with fennel, lime and orange

Serves 4 as a starter

500g very fresh grey mullet fillet, pin-boned and skinned
1 tbsp olive oil, plus extra to finish
2 red onions, peeled and sliced
2 red chillies, halved, deseeded and sliced
2 garlic cloves, peeled and finely chopped
2 oranges
Juice of 2 limes
2 fennel bulbs, tough outer layer removed
4 radishes, trimmed
2 tbsp coriander leaves, finely sliced
Sea salt

Place a small pan over a medium heat and add the olive oil. When it is hot, add one of the sliced onions and sweat for 2 minutes. Next, add the chillies and garlic and sweat for a further 2 minutes. Transfer to a blender and blitz well to a paste. Allow this chilli paste to cool.

Soak the other sliced onion in cold water to cover for 5 minutes. Drain, then dry on kitchen paper. Put the onion into a bowl, cover and place in the fridge until needed.

Slice the fish thinly, season with salt and place in a bowl. Leave to stand for 5 minutes.

Meanwhile, squeeze the juice from one of the oranges. Cut away the peel and pith from the other orange and cut out the segments from between the membranes; cut these into smaller pieces.

Drizzle the orange and lime juices over the fish and mix well. Cover with a plate and place in the fridge for 20 minutes. During this time the fish will effectively 'cook' in the citrus juice.

In the meantime, slice the fennel very thinly, ideally on a mandoline, then place it in a bowl of cold water to firm and crisp up. Do the same with the radishes.

When the fish is ready, drain off the juice, then add 1 tbsp chilli paste and toss to mix. Drain the fennel and radishes and add them to the fish along with the orange pieces, red onion slices and sliced coriander. Toss to combine and taste for seasoning, adding more salt if needed.

To serve, divide between individual plates or shallow bowls and drizzle with a little olive oil.

When mackerel is around, I can't get enough of it and I always try to find new ways of serving it. Once autumn arrives mackerel is plentiful, as are cabbages and apples, so it makes sense to bring them together. Here, crunchy red cabbage and crisp apple complement soft, rich mackerel and the cider tones from the salad cream and pickle marry them together perfectly.

Pickled mackerel with red cabbage, apple and cider

Serves 4

4 very fresh mackerel, filleted
  and pin-boned
1 tbsp olive oil
1 red onion, peeled and thinly
  sliced
½ red cabbage, outer leaves
  removed, thinly sliced
2 Braeburn apples, peeled and
  grated
Sea salt

For the pickling liquor

200ml cider vinegar
200ml cider
50g caster sugar
1 garlic clove, peeled and
  crushed
2 thyme sprigs
2 bay leaves

For the salad cream

2 egg yolks
1 tsp English mustard
2 tsp caster sugar
2 tbsp cider vinegar
2 tbsp cider
350ml olive oil
50ml double cream
2 tbsp dill leaves, chopped,
  plus extra sprigs to garnish

For the pickling liquor, put all the ingredients into a pan and heat to dissolve the sugar, then bring to the boil, lower the heat and simmer for 2 minutes. Add a pinch of salt.

Lay the mackerel fillets side by side in a dish that holds them snugly in one layer. Pour on the pickling liquor and cover with greaseproof paper, pushing it down onto the surface with a saucer to keep everything submerged. Leave to stand for 2 hours: the fish will effectively 'cook' in the liquor. (It can be kept in the liquor for up to 2 days.)

Meanwhile, heat a small frying pan and add the olive oil. When the oil is hot, add the red onion and sweat for 2–3 minutes. Season with salt and transfer the onion to a tray to cool.

To make the salad cream, put the egg yolks, mustard, sugar, cider vinegar and cider into a bowl and whisk together for 1 minute. Now gradually add the olive oil, drop by drop to begin with, then in a thin, steady stream until it is all incorporated. To finish, slowly whisk in the cream and season with salt to taste. Transfer to a bowl and stir through the chopped dill. Cover and refrigerate until required.

To serve, combine the onion, red cabbage and apples in a bowl. Mix well and season with salt to taste.

Remove the mackerel fillets from the pickle. Spoon some salad cream onto each of 4 plates and pile the red cabbage mixture into the centre. Arrange the mackerel fillets on top. Add a sprinkle of sea salt and finish with a few dill sprigs.

We go herring mad when they come into season in Cornwall and prepare them in all sorts of ways. Pickling is one of my favourite treatments and this recipe is incredibly simple. Just make sure your herring are top quality and really fresh. Feel free to change the flavourings, if you like, and don't worry about the small bones – they disintegrate in the pickling mix.

Pickled herrings, red onion, orange and tarragon dressing

Serves 4 as a starter

8 very fresh herring, gutted, scaled and filleted
3 shallots, peeled and finely sliced
3 garlic cloves, peeled and crushed
1 tsp dried chilli flakes
4 tsp fennel seeds
2 bay leaves
500ml white wine vinegar
200g caster sugar
3 oranges
200ml orange oil (see page 216)
2 red onions, peeled, halved and thinly sliced
4 tbsp tarragon leaves, chopped
Sea salt

Lay the herring fillets side by side in a suitable plastic container that is big enough to hold them snugly covered by the pickling liquor.

Put the shallots, garlic, chilli flakes, fennel seeds and bay leaves into a pan. Add the wine vinegar, sugar and the finely grated zest of one of the oranges. Bring to a simmer and simmer for 2 minutes, then add 4 tsp salt. Remove from the heat and allow to cool.

Once cooled, pour the pickling mix over the herring fillets and cover with greaseproof paper, pushing it down onto the surface to keep the fish submerged before adding the lid. Place in the fridge and leave for 24 hours before eating.

Take the fish out of the fridge at least an hour before serving to bring it back to room temperature. Cut the peel and pith from all 3 oranges and cut out the segments from between the membranes.

For the dressing, measure 50ml of the pickling liquor and mix it with the orange oil, orange segments, red onion slices and chopped tarragon. Season with salt to taste.

Lay the herring fillets on a large platter and spoon over the orange, red onion and tarragon dressing. Serve with sourdough and salted butter.

Gurnard has a lovely meaty quality and a unique flavour that I love. It can handle big flavours too, including my red pepper ketchup. This dish will sit quite happily in the fridge for up to 3 days. Just make sure you take it out of the fridge a few hours before serving to bring the flavours alive.

Soused gurnard, red pepper ketchup, rocket and black olive salad

Serves 4 as a main course

4 very fresh small gurnard, about 600g each, or 2 larger fish, filleted and pin-boned
250ml olive oil
2 onions, peeled and sliced
2 red peppers, cored, deseeded and sliced
75ml red wine vinegar
2 garlic cloves, peeled and sliced
2 rosemary sprigs
A handful of flat-leaf parsley, leaves picked and chopped
Sea salt

For the red pepper ketchup

50ml olive oil
2 red onions, peeled and chopped
3 red peppers, peeled, cored, deseeded and chopped
2 garlic cloves, peeled and sliced
1 red chilli, deseeded and chopped
500g ripe tomatoes, chopped
75g caster sugar
1 rosemary sprig, leaves picked and chopped
100ml white wine vinegar
100ml balsamic vinegar
50g tin good quality anchovy fillets in oil, drained

For the rocket and olive salad

2 handfuls of rocket leaves
100g black olives, pitted
Finely grated zest and juice of 1 lemon
A drizzle of olive oil

Heat a large non-stick frying pan and add a drizzle of olive oil. When hot, add the gurnard fillets and fry until the skin side is golden. Turn the fillets over in the pan, count to 30 and then remove to an oven dish.

Add a little more oil to the frying pan, then add the onions and peppers and sweat for 4–5 minutes until the peppers soften and start to collapse. Add the remaining olive oil, wine vinegar, garlic and rosemary and bring to a simmer. Season with salt and pour over the fish fillets. Cover with greaseproof paper, pushing it down onto the surface to keep the fish submerged. Leave to souse for at least 2 hours.

To make the ketchup, place a large pan over a medium heat and add the olive oil. When hot, add the onions, peppers, garlic and red chilli and cook for 4 minutes until the onions are translucent. Add the tomatoes with the sugar and rosemary and cook for 15 minutes until they have broken down. Add both vinegars and the anchovies and let bubble until the liquor becomes syrupy.

Transfer the mixture to a blender or food processor and blitz until smooth, then pass through a sieve into a bowl. Taste for seasoning and adjust with salt to taste. Cover and leave to cool. (The ketchup will keep fine in a sealed container in the fridge for up to a week; it can also be frozen.)

For the salad, toss the rocket, olives and lemon zest together and dress with lemon juice, olive oil and salt to taste. Arrange on 4 plates.

Lift the gurnard out of the sousing liquid and share the fillets between the plates. Pass the sousing liquid through a sieve into a bowl. Transfer the peppers from the sieve to another bowl, add the chopped parsley and mix well. Divide the peppers between the plates.

Finish with a drizzle of sousing liquid and a generous spoonful of the red pepper ketchup.

I like to cook Dover sole on the bone, so the fillets keep their natural shape. If you fillet the fish first, the fillets tend to shrink quite a lot during cooking. Sousing Dover sole is unusual, but I find the acidity is welcome and it adds more depth of flavour. The mushrooms and seaweed marry well with the vinegar and wine, but nothing outshines the star of the show, the Dover sole.

Hot soused Dover sole with mushroom and seaweed dressing

Serves 4 as a main course

4 Dover sole, about 500g
   each, skinned and heads
   removed
100ml olive oil
2 red onions, peeled and
   sliced
300g mixed mushrooms,
   cleaned
4 garlic cloves, peeled and
   finely chopped
100ml sherry vinegar
100ml white wine
2 tbsp dried seaweed flakes
2 tbsp chopped flat-leaf
   parsley
Sea salt and freshly ground
   black pepper

Preheat your oven to 200°C/Fan 185°C/Gas 6.

Heat a large frying pan and add a drizzle of olive oil. When hot, add the red onions and cook for 3–4 minutes until they start to soften. Scatter the onions in a roasting tray big enough to hold the fish (or use 2 or 4 smaller trays).

Wipe out the frying pan and heat again. When hot, add another drizzle of oil. Toss in the mushrooms and cook for 3 minutes, then add the garlic and continue to cook for another 2 minutes. Season with salt and pepper and add to the onions in the tray(s).

Wipe out the frying pan again. Season the fish all over with salt and pepper. Heat the pan and add a drizzle of olive oil. When hot, add the Dover soles and fry for 2 minutes. Turn the fish over and cook for a further 2 minutes.

Mix the sherry vinegar and wine together and add to the pan to deglaze. Remove from the heat and add the seaweed and any remaining olive oil. Transfer the fish to the tray(s), spooning some of the mushrooms and onions on top of them, then pour over the juices from the frying pan. Bake for 8–10 minutes until cooked.

Sprinkle the chopped parsley over the cooked fish, then carefully transfer to warmed plates. Spoon the mushrooms, onions and juices over the fish. I like to serve this simply with boiled new potatoes and seasonal green vegetables.

The most common hot marinated dish is the classic escabeche, which I adore. The technique works well with lots of fish – you just need to get the balance of acidity and heat right. As lemon sole fillets are thin, they are well suited, because they readily take on the acidity of the marinade and 'cook' quickly. Megrim sole and small plaice are equally suitable. This is a great dish for two, but you can easily double or triple the quantities to serve more.

Hot marinated lemon sole with pickled onions and grapes

Serves 2 as a main course

2 lemon sole, about 500g
  each, scaled and filleted

For the pickling marinade

Olive oil for cooking
12 baby white onions, peeled
  and left whole
2 celery sticks, de-stringed
  (with a peeler) and finely
  sliced
2 garlic cloves, halved and
  germ removed, finely
  chopped
1 green chilli, halved,
  deseeded and finely
  chopped
1 rosemary sprig, leaves
  picked and finely chopped
400g tin cannellini or other
  white beans, drained
75ml verjus
100ml white wine
250ml fish stock (see
  page 218)
Sea salt and freshly ground
  black pepper

To assemble and serve

1 tbsp chopped chives
1 tbsp chopped flat-leaf
  parsley
20 red seedless grapes, halved
A drizzle of extra virgin
  olive oil

To prepare the pickling marinade, heat a large saucepan over a medium heat and add a generous drizzle of olive oil. When the oil is hot, add the baby onions and cook for 4–5 minutes, turning occasionally to colour evenly.

When the onions are nice and golden, add the celery, garlic, chilli and rosemary, and cook for 2 minutes. Add the white beans to the pan and cook for another 2 minutes, then add the verjus and cook for a further 2 minutes. Pour in the wine and stock, bring to the boil and season with salt and pepper. Remove from the heat.

Lay the lemon sole fillets in a dish large enough to hold the fish flat and level. Bring the marinade back to a simmer, then carefully pour it over the fish. Leave to stand for 10 minutes.

Just before serving, scatter the chives, parsley and grapes over the fish and finish with a drizzle of olive oil over the top.

In a pickle   83

BOWL
FOOD

When asparagus is at its best in the UK, so are the prized male 'cock' crabs and it makes perfect sense to pair these two delicacies. The result is magic and one of my all-time favourites. I finish this simple dish with a drizzle of emerald green seaweed oil, which I make from the gutweed we gather around the beaches close to the restaurants. If you find it hard to get hold of, make a parsley or chive oil following the same method instead.

Chilled asparagus soup, crabmeat and seaweed oil

Serves 4 as a starter

250g white crabmeat (from a 1.5kg freshly cooked crab)
Olive oil for cooking and serving
2 shallots, peeled and finely sliced
1 potato, peeled and thinly sliced
1 litre vegetable stock (see page 218)
600g asparagus, woody parts removed, thinly sliced
300ml double cream
A squeeze of lemon juice
Sea salt and freshly ground black pepper

For the seaweed oil

2 large handfuls of gutweed, thoroughly washed and picked
A large handful of spinach leaves
500ml sunflower oil

To prepare the seaweed oil, bring a pan of water to the boil, add the seaweed and spinach and blanch for 30 seconds. Remove and plunge into a bowl of iced water to cool. Drain thoroughly and squeeze out all excess water. Tip into a blender, add the oil and blend thoroughly. Transfer to a bowl or jug, cover and refrigerate until needed.

To make the soup, heat a large saucepan over a medium heat and add a drizzle of olive oil. When hot, add the shallots and potato and cook for 2 minutes. Pour in the stock, bring to the boil, then lower the heat and simmer for 10 minutes until the potato is cooked.

Add the asparagus and cook for 1 minute. Meanwhile, set a bowl (large enough to hold the soup) over another bowl filled with ice.

Pour the cream into the soup, bring back to the boil and season with salt and pepper to taste. Let the mixture cool slightly then transfer to a blender and blitz until smooth. Pour the soup into the bowl (over ice) to cool it quickly.

When the soup is cold, cover and place in the fridge until ready to serve. Chill 4 soup bowls too.

When ready to serve, check the white crabmeat for any fragments of shell or cartilage. Divide most of the crabmeat between the chilled soup bowls, holding a little back for the garnish. Season the crabmeat and add a drizzle of olive oil and a squeeze of lemon juice.

Give the soup a good stir and check the seasoning again. Share the soup equally between the bowls and top each one with some crabmeat. Finish with a drizzle of seaweed oil.

One of the best memories I have of Singapore is the food markets and stalls. I love the fact that you can sit in the market and try all the different foods that are on offer. The prawn noodle soup I tasted there was something else. I wasn't quite sure how they made it, but after a few trials I think this is pretty close... it tastes good anyway.

Prawn noodle soup

Serves 4 as a starter

For the stock

500g raw Atlantic prawns in
  shell, plus extra shells and
  heads (see below)
A generous drizzle of
  sunflower oil
4 garlic cloves, peeled and
  sliced
1 litre water

For the soup

1 tbsp sunflower oil
200g piece of smoked streaky
  bacon, cut into lardons
4 spring onions, trimmed,
  white and green parts
  separated and sliced
2 red chillies, deseeded and
  thinly sliced
2 garlic cloves, peeled and
  finely chopped
5 tbsp fish sauce
2 tbsp white wine
300g rice noodles
16 raw tiger prawns, shelled
  and deveined (keep shells
  and heads for stock)
2 pak choi, sliced into strips
70g bean sprouts
Sea salt and freshly ground
  black pepper

To make the prawn stock, heat the oil in a sauté pan, then add the garlic and cook until golden. Add the prawns (plus the extra shells and heads from the shelled prawns for the soup) and cook until they turn orangey red all over. Crush the prawns with the back of a spoon, then add the water and bring to the boil. Add a good pinch of salt and simmer for 25 minutes. Strain through a sieve into a bowl and set aside.

To make the soup, heat the oil in a large saucepan. When it is hot, add the bacon, white spring onions, chillies and garlic. Sweat for 5 minutes, stirring every so often.

Now pour in the prawn stock, bring to a simmer and cook gently for 10 minutes. Stir in the fish sauce and wine. Season with salt and pepper to taste.

Tip the rice noodles into the pan and cook for 3 minutes. Add the prawns and pak choi and cook for a further 2 minutes until they turn orangey red. Finally, add the green spring onions and bean sprouts.

To serve, ladle the soup into 4 warmed bowls, dividing the noodles, beansprouts, pak choi and prawns evenly. Serve at once.

This is a brilliant soup to make in late summer when fresh sweetcorn is at its best. It proved a real crowd pleaser when I served little bowls of it in the restaurant as a pre-dinner *amuse bouche*. Beautiful seared scallops complement the sweetcorn flavour perfectly, while the pickled red onions cut the richness and stop the soup becoming too sweet.

Sweetcorn soup with scallops and pickled red onions

Serves 4 as a starter or light lunch

12 fresh scallops, shelled and cleaned (roes retained if in good condition)
4 corn on the cobs
Olive oil for cooking and to drizzle
75g unsalted butter
4 tsp chopped coriander leaves
Sea salt and freshly ground black pepper

For the pickled red onions
2 small red onions, peeled and finely sliced into rings
100ml red wine
100ml red wine vinegar
100g caster sugar
100ml water

Cut the sweetcorn kernels from the cobs, by standing the cobs upright on a board and cutting downwards with a sharp knife.

Heat a drizzle of olive oil and the butter in a large saucepan over a medium heat, then add the sweetcorn. Cook for 15–20 minutes, stirring every couple of minutes so the corn toasts at the edges but does not burn. Pour in enough water to barely cover it and bring to a simmer. Cook for about 15 minutes until the sweetcorn is tender.

Meanwhile, prepare the pickled onions. Put the red onion slices into a bowl. Heat the wine, wine vinegar, sugar and water in a small pan to dissolve the sugar, then bring to the boil. Add a pinch of salt and pour this pickling liquor over the onion slices. Cover and leave to cool.

When the corn is tender, blitz with the cooking liquor in a blender, or using a stick blender in the pan, for 3–4 minutes until smooth. Return to the pan (if necessary) and taste for seasoning, adding salt and pepper as you like. If the soup is too thick, add a little more water. Leave over a low heat while you cook the scallops.

Heat a large non-stick pan frying pan over a medium heat and add a drizzle of olive oil. Season the scallops with salt and place, one by one, in the hot pan, remembering where you placed the first one. Cook for 2 minutes until golden, then carefully flip them over in the same order you placed them in the pan. Take off the heat and allow the scallops to finish cooking in the residual heat.

Drain the pickled onions (you can save the pickling liquor to use again).

Bring the soup back to a simmer and divide between 4 warmed bowls. Place 3 scallops in each bowl and add some pickled red onion slices and a scattering of chopped coriander. Finish with a drizzle of olive oil and serve immediately.

I make lots of different chowders, especially in winter, as I love the hearty and warming feeling it gives you when you eat one. This is a favourite: the salty clams and almost crunchy texture of the prawns are great with the rich broth. I like to add plenty of fresh herbs and a splash of verjus at the end to lift the flavours. Feel free to change any of the ingredients, but stick to the technique – it works so well.

Clam and prawn chowder

Serves 4 as a starter or light lunch

16 raw prawns, shelled and heads removed (keep for cooking) and deveined
2 large handfuls of live surf, Venus or carpet shell clams
800ml whole milk
200ml double cream
2 garlic cloves, peeled, halved (germ removed) and finely chopped
300g potatoes, such as Maris Piper, peeled and thinly sliced
125ml verjus
50ml cold-pressed rapeseed oil, plus extra to drizzle
2 large banana shallots or 6 ordinary shallots, peeled and finely chopped
1 leek, outer layer removed, halved lengthways, washed well and finely sliced
2 celery sticks, de-stringed (with a peeler) and cut into 1cm dice
1 small celeriac, peeled and cut into 1cm dice
1 red chilli, halved, deseeded and finely sliced
100ml dry cider
500ml fish stock
½ handful of dill, leaves picked and finely chopped
½ handful of tarragon, leaves picked and finely chopped
Sea salt and freshly ground black pepper

To make the chowder, pour the milk and cream into a large pan and add the garlic and potatoes. Tie the prawn heads and shells in muslin and add to the pan. Bring to a simmer and simmer for 10 minutes or until the potatoes are soft.

Meanwhile, heat another large pan with a tight-fitting lid over a high heat. When hot, add the clams and 100ml verjus. Immediately put the lid on and steam for 3 minutes until the shells open. Tip the contents of the pan into a colander set over a bowl, to catch the juices. Set aside.

Wipe the pan clean and place over a medium heat. When it is hot, add the rapeseed oil, followed by the shallots, leek, celery, celeriac and chilli. Cook, stirring occasionally, for 5 minutes without colouring. Now pour in the cider and fish stock and bring to a simmer. Cook for 10 minutes until the vegetables are softened.

In the meantime, remove and discard the muslin bag of prawn shells from the chowder pan, then tip the contents of the pan into a blender and blitz until smooth. Add to the vegetables and stock, along with the reserved clam juice. Stir and check the seasoning, adding salt and pepper to taste.

Pick three-quarters of the clams out of their shells, leaving the rest in. Bring the chowder to a simmer. Add the prawns and cook for 2 minutes, until they turn pink, then add all the clams, herbs and the remaining splash of verjus.

Turn off the heat and stir the chowder gently to avoid breaking the clam shells. Ladle into a warmed tureen or soup bowls and drizzle some rapeseed oil over the surface. Serve straight away.

This Japanese style broth may not be authentic, but I can whip it up in minutes at home and it tastes so good. The combination of red mullet and East Asian mushrooms is amazing. You should be able to buy dashi flakes quite easily, but shiso might be a little more difficult to find. Shiso is like a Japanese basil, so you could use basil in its place. If you don't have time to make the shiso oil, add a splash of toasted sesame oil instead.

Red mullet and mushroom miso broth with shiso oil

Serves 4 as a hearty starter or light lunch

2 red mullet, about 500g each, scaled, filleted and pin-boned
50ml light rapeseed oil, plus extra for oiling
1 litre water
1 tbsp instant dashi flakes
2 tbsp white miso paste
50g dried ceps
6 spring onions, finely sliced (white and green parts separated)
50g shimeji mushrooms
50g eryngii (or oyster) mushrooms
75g shiitake mushrooms
1 garlic clove, peeled and finely chopped
Juice of 1 lime
300g packet dried udon noodles
200g tofu, cut into cubes
Sea salt and freshly ground black pepper

For the shiso oil
2 handfuls of shiso leaves
100g spinach leaves
50g fresh ginger, peeled and finely chopped
2 tsp caster sugar
200ml light rapeseed oil

First make the shiso oil. Have a bowl of iced water ready. Bring a pan of salted water to the boil, add the shiso and spinach leaves and cook for 1 minute. Remove immediately and plunge into the iced water to cool quickly. Drain and squeeze out the excess water.

Put the shiso and spinach into a blender and add the ginger, sugar, rapeseed oil and some salt and pepper. Blitz for 2 minutes, then pour into a jug or bowl, cover and refrigerate.

Preheat your grill to high. Oil a grill tray and sprinkle with salt and pepper. Slice each red mullet fillet into 2 equal pieces, lay on the grill tray and turn to coat in the oil and seasoning, then place skin side up. Set aside.

Put the water and dashi flakes into a saucepan over a medium heat and bring to a simmer, then whisk in the miso paste and dried ceps. Cover the pan, remove from the heat and leave to stand for 10 minutes.

Meanwhile, heat a frying pan over a medium heat and add the rapeseed oil. When hot, add the white spring onions and all of the mushrooms. Cook for 3 minutes, then add the garlic. Season with salt and pepper to taste and add the lime juice, stirring to deglaze. Remove from the heat and put to one side.

Strain the miso liquor through a fine sieve into a clean pan, discarding the ceps, and bring to the boil. Add the noodles and cook for 2 minutes until they are just tender.

Cook the fish under the grill for 2 minutes. Add the green spring onions and tofu to the broth and heat for 1 minute.

Ladle the broth, noodles and mushrooms into 4 warmed bowls, sharing them equally. Add 2 pieces of red mullet to each bowl and finish with a drizzle of shiso oil. Serve at once.

Smoked haddock makes such a lovely, comforting soup. It marries perfectly with egg and bacon in this hearty chowder for a nourishing lunch or supper, or even brunch, if you fancy. It's worth buying really good quality smoked haddock – avoid that cheap, bright yellow dyed stuff.

Smoked haddock soup with poached egg and pancetta

Serves 4 as a hearty starter or light lunch

600g smoked haddock fillet, skinned, pin-boned and diced (trimmings saved)
200ml fish stock (see page 218)
200ml milk
100ml double cream
Olive oil for cooking and to drizzle
2 white onions, peeled and finely chopped
1 celery stick, de-stringed (with a peeler) and thinly sliced
2 garlic cloves, peeled and finely chopped
1 large potato, peeled and diced
6 thin slices of pancetta
100ml white wine vinegar
4 large eggs
Sea salt and freshly ground black pepper

Pour the fish stock, milk and cream into a saucepan and add the smoked haddock trimmings. Bring to the boil and then take off the heat.

Place another large saucepan over a medium heat and add a little olive oil. When hot, add the onions, celery and garlic. Cook, stirring occasionally, for 4 minutes, then stir in the diced potato. Strain the creamy milk and stock mixture over the vegetables and bring to a simmer. Cook gently for 8–10 minutes until the potatoes are soft. Let cool slightly then transfer to a blender and blitz until smooth.

Meanwhile, preheat your grill to high and lay the pancetta on a grill tray. Bring a large pan of water to a simmer with the wine vinegar added.

Place the pancetta under the grill and cook until crispy. Carefully crack the eggs into the simmering water. (There is no need to stir the water – if your eggs are fresh they will form a nice shape instantly.) Poach the eggs for 3 minutes.

Meanwhile, add the smoked haddock to the soup and cook gently for 2 minutes. Remove from the heat and taste for seasoning, adding salt and pepper if you wish.

Cut the grilled pancetta in half. When the poached eggs are ready, drain them on kitchen paper.

Share the soup equally between 4 warmed bowls. Place a poached egg in each bowl, season with pepper and surround with the crispy pancetta. Add a generous drizzle of olive oil and serve straight away.

If you enjoy fragrant Thai flavours, you will love this dish. The classic Thai aromatics really help to bring the flavours of the seafood alive. I've used razor clams and queenie scallops, but prawns or any other shellfish will work. The chilli oil is a nice finishing touch if you like a bit of heat.

Razor clam and scallop soup with coconut, lemongrass and chilli

Serves 4 as a hearty starter or light lunch

2kg live razor clams
20 queenie scallops, cleaned, or 8 standard scallops, cleaned and halved
50ml sunflower oil
2 red onions, peeled and finely sliced
3 lemongrass stalks, tough outer layers removed, finely chopped
50g fresh ginger, peeled and finely grated
2 garlic cloves, peeled and finely chopped
2 bird's eye chillies, deseeded and finely chopped
2 x 400ml tins coconut milk
2 tbsp fish sauce
3 tbsp lime juice
A handful of coriander, leaves picked
2 handfuls of baby spinach leaves
Chilli oil (see page 216) to finish

Check that your clams are alive and closed; discard any that are open. Place a large pan with a tight-fitting lid over a high heat. When hot, add the clams with a mugful of water. Immediately put the lid on and steam the clams for 2 minutes until the shells open. Tip the contents of the pan into a colander set over a bowl, to catch the juices. Leave to cool.

Wipe the pan clean and place over a medium heat. When hot, add the oil, followed by the onions, lemongrass, ginger, garlic and chillies. Cook, stirring, for 2 minutes, then pour in the coconut milk and bring to a simmer. Allow to simmer for 5 minutes.

Meanwhile, prepare the clams. Remove the meat from the shells, then cut away and discard the sandy and black parts. Slice the meat into even-sized pieces and set aside. Pass the clam juice through a fine sieve into a bowl and reserve.

Add the fish sauce, lime juice, coriander, spinach and strained clam juice to the coconut liquor and bring back to the boil. Stir in the scallops and return to a simmer. Remove from the heat and stir in the razor clam meat; the scallops will finish cooking in the residual heat.

Ladle the soup equally into 4 warmed bowls. Drizzle with a little chilli oil and serve, with crusty bread.

I often make this quick and healthy soup at home – even the kids like it! The smoky oiliness of mackerel is great with fresh tasting parsley and spinach, and the horseradish adds a lovely kick. You can vary the leafy green veg and/or herb if you like. If you want to make the soup in advance, chill it down quickly in a bowl over ice to retain that lovely green colour and fresh flavour.

Parsley soup, smoked mackerel, horseradish and lemon oil

Serves 4 as a lunch

6 smoked mackerel fillets
50ml light olive oil, plus extra to drizzle
50ml unsalted butter
2 banana shallots, peeled and finely chopped
3 garlic cloves, peeled, halved (germ removed) and finely chopped
2 large Maris Piper potatoes, peeled and finely sliced
1.5 litres fish or vegetable stock (see page 218)
2 tbsp creamed horseradish
3 handfuls of flat-leaf parsley, leaves picked
100g baby spinach leaves
Sea salt and freshly ground black pepper
Horseradish and lemon oil (see page 216), to finish

Cut each smoked mackerel fillet into 3 pieces.

Heat a large saucepan over a medium heat and add the 50ml olive oil with the butter. When hot, add the shallots and garlic and cook for 2 minutes until translucent. Now add the potatoes with some salt and pepper. Cook, stirring constantly, for 2 minutes.

Pour in the stock, bring to a simmer and cook until the potato is soft, about 8–10 minutes. If you don't cook it enough, the soup will have a grainy texture. Tip the contents of the pan into a blender and add the creamed horseradish.

Wipe the pan clean, return to the heat and add a drizzle of olive oil. When hot, add the parsley and spinach and cook until wilted.

Tip the parsley and spinach into the blender and blend until smooth (see note). Return the soup to the pan, heat until piping hot, then taste and adjust the seasoning if necessary.

Divide the soup equally between 4 warmed bowls and top with the pieces of smoked mackerel. Finish with a drizzle of horseradish and lemon oil.

Note Be very careful when blending a hot soup, as hot air builds up in the jug and will burst out of the top if it is not released. I suggest you pulse it slowly at first with a cloth over the top, then as the soup begins to blend down, blitz in the usual way.

When I opened Outlaw's Fish Kitchen in Port Isaac I wanted to do a new mussel dish that screamed out 'Cornwall!' and showed off our fantastic mussels. This is that dish: a marriage of cider, apple, sage and clotted cream. Flavours that to me work wonders with the plumpest and juiciest mussels. A simple, quick dish that really impresses every time I cook it.

Mussels with sage, cider and clotted cream

Serves 2 as a starter or light lunch

1kg live mussels
A drizzle of cold-pressed rapeseed oil
2 small white onions, peeled and sliced
8 sage leaves, finely sliced
100g Cornish clotted cream
200ml medium dry cider
1 Braeburn apple, peeled, cored and diced
2 tbsp chopped flat-leaf parsley
Freshly ground black pepper

Wash the mussels and pull away the hairy beard attached to one end of the shell. Discard any mussels that are open and refuse to close when pinched back together, and any that have damaged shells.

Place a large pan that has a tight-fitting lid over a high heat. When it is hot, add the oil, followed by the onions. Cook, stirring frequently, for 3 minutes, until they soften and singe at the edge.

Add the mussels, sage and clotted cream, cover and cook for 30 seconds. Lift the lid, pour in the cider and re-cover. Cook for 3 minutes. Lift the lid to check if the mussels are open. If not, put the lid back on and cook for a further 30 seconds, or until all, or most of the mussels are open.

Add the diced apple and chopped parsley and toss to mix. Divide the mussels between 2 warmed bowls and pour over the tasty liquor. Serve at once, with crusty bread and butter.

This dish is very popular when it goes on any of our menus. The scallops we get are hand-dived off the south coast of Cornwall and have a unique texture and taste. Our supply is dependent on the weather, so we treasure them as a luxury ingredient. Their incomparable sweet flavour and beautiful texture really shine through in this simple dish.

Pan-fried scallops, creamed chicory, orange and tarragon dressing

Serves 4 as a starter or light lunch

16–20 fresh scallops, shelled and cleaned (roes retained if in good condition)
Olive oil for cooking
Sea salt and freshly ground black pepper

For the chicory

2 chicory heads, outer leaves removed, shredded
50ml olive oil
75g unsalted butter
30g caster sugar
1 white onion, peeled and finely sliced
Finely grated zest and juice of ½ orange
150ml double cream

For the orange and tarragon dressing

1 orange
8 tbsp extra virgin olive oil

To finish

3 tsp chopped tarragon

For the chicory, heat a large frying pan over a medium-high heat and add the olive oil, butter and sugar. When hot, add the onion and cook, stirring occasionally, for 2 minutes. Now add the chicory and cook for 2 minutes, turning from time to time.

Turn the heat down under the chicory to medium and add the orange zest and juice. Let the juice bubble away, then add the cream. Bring to a simmer and let simmer for 5 minutes. Remove from the heat.

Meanwhile, for the dressing, cut the peel and pith from the orange and cut out the segments from the membranes over a bowl to catch any juice. Slice the orange segments and place in a bowl with the extra virgin olive oil and some salt and pepper. Set aside.

To cook the scallops, heat a non-stick pan until very hot. Season the scallops with salt and drizzle some olive oil into the pan. Carefully place the scallops in the pan, one by one, remembering where you placed the first one. Turn the heat down to medium and cook for 2 minutes. Now flip the scallops over in the same order you placed them in the pan and cook for a further minute. Take the pan off the heat and allow the scallops to finish cooking in the residual heat.

To serve, warm up the creamed chicory if need be, then taste and correct the seasoning. Divide the chicory between 4 warmed plates or shallow bowls and top each serving with 4 or 5 scallops. Add a good drizzle of orange dressing and sprinkle with the chopped tarragon. Serve warm.

On a trip to Singapore I became a little obsessed with crab dishes and set about recreating the exciting street food I had eaten. The crabs we have in the UK are different to those in Asia, which are smaller and have softer shells. Still, it's easy enough to flavour our crab in the same way and cook it in a similar fashion. You need plenty of bread and beer with this scrumptious spicy dish.

Crab with tomatoes, chilli, green peppercorns and herbs

Serves 6

3 live brown crabs, about
   1.5kg each

For the sauce
100ml olive oil
3 white onions, peeled and
   chopped
2 bunches of spring onions,
   cut into fine julienne, white
   and green parts separated
6 garlic cloves, peeled and
   finely chopped
2 green chillies, sliced (seeds
   left in)
14 ripe plum tomatoes,
   chopped
150ml verjus
600ml white wine
2 tbsp green peppercorns
2 tbsp chopped tarragon
2 tbsp chopped chives
3 tbsp chopped parsley
Sea salt and freshly ground
   black pepper

To make the sauce, heat the olive oil in a large frying pan over a medium heat. When hot, add the onions, white spring onions, garlic and chillies and cook for 4–5 minutes until the onions are soft and starting to colour. Add the tomatoes and cook, stirring occasionally, for 4–5 minutes.

Add the verjus and cook for a further 5 minutes, then pour in the wine and let it bubble to reduce down. Add the green peppercorns and season with salt and pepper to taste. Simmer for another couple of minutes, then remove from the heat and set aside.

To cook the crabs, bring a very large pan of very salty water (30g salt to 1 litre water) to the boil. When it is almost boiling, lay each crab on its back on a board. Lift the flap near the bottom and plunge a large cook's knife into the point underneath to kill the crab instantly. Immediately plunge the crabs into the boiling water and cook for 12 minutes.

Lift the cooked crabs out onto a large tray and leave until cool enough to handle. Hold the crab in both hands and use your thumbs to push the body up and out of the hard top shell. Twist off the claws and legs and crack them. Remove and discard the dead man's fingers, stomach sac and hard membranes from the body shell. Now, cut the body in half and then into quarters.

To finish the dish, heat the sauce and add the green spring onions and chopped herbs. When the sauce comes to a simmer, taste for seasoning and adjust as necessary. Add all of the crab, give it a gentle stir and warm through for a couple of minutes.

To serve, carefully tip the contents of the pan into a large warmed serving dish. Place in the centre of the table with finger bowls, spoons, beer and bread.

This risotto is versatile. I love the pairing of cockles and seaweed, but you could use any seafood in place of the cockles, or even a mixture of seafood if you wish. Similarly, any good seaweed will work, even crushed nori sheets that you buy for sushi – it just needs to be dehydrated and blitzed, to tenderise in the risotto. Adding the hot stock little by little and stirring continuously helps to release the starch from the rice grains, giving you that wonderful, creamy end result. Have all the ingredients prepared before you start, so you can concentrate on the stirring.

Cockle and seaweed risotto

Serves 4

1kg live cockles
150g granary or sourdough
  bread, crusts removed and
  torn into pieces
50ml light olive oil, plus extra
  to drizzle
1 litre vegetable or fish stock
  (see page 218)
50g unsalted butter
1 large white onion, peeled
  and finely chopped
1 fennel bulb, tough outer
  layer removed, finely
  chopped
2 garlic cloves, peeled, halved
  (germ removed) and finely
  chopped
240g carnaroli risotto rice
50ml white wine vinegar
100ml dry white wine
2 tbsp dried seaweed flakes,
  plus an extra 1 tsp to
  garnish
100g Parmesan, freshly grated
8 spring onions, trimmed and
  thinly sliced
A handful of tarragon, leaves
  picked and chopped
A handful of dill, leaves
  picked and finely chopped
Grated zest of 1 lime
Sea salt and freshly ground
  black pepper

Preheat your oven to 200°C/Fan 185°C/Gas 6. Put the pieces of bread on an oven tray, drizzle with olive oil and season with salt and pepper. Bake in the oven for 10 minutes until golden and crispy.

Meanwhile, bring the stock to a simmer in a saucepan over a low heat and keep it at a steady simmer.

Place another large heavy-based saucepan over a medium heat and add the olive oil and butter. When the butter starts to bubble, add the onion, fennel and garlic and cook for 3 minutes until the onion is translucent. Add the rice and cook, stirring, for 2 minutes.

Tip the crisp bread pieces onto a plate lined with kitchen paper to drain; set aside.

Pour the wine vinegar and wine into the rice pan and cook, stirring, until reduced right down to almost nothing, about 3 minutes. Add the 2 tbsp dried seaweed. Now add the stock, a ladleful at a time and cook, stirring slowly and continuously with a wooden spoon, for 12 minutes. Allow each ladleful of stock to be fully absorbed before you add the next.

Next add the cockles along with another ladleful of stock and cook for 2 minutes, or until the cockles start to open. Immediately add the grated Parmesan, spring onions and chopped herbs and turn off the heat.

Give the risotto a careful stir and share between 4 warmed plates. Scatter over the crisp bread pieces and lime zest, and finish with a sprinkling of seaweed. Serve immediately.

Fish stew exists all around the globe. Where you are, or where you live, determines what goes in. I like to use fish with a firm texture that will give a real depth of flavour. Roasting the fish heads and bones – and cooking the vegetables in the way I do here – really intensifies the flavours. The scallops are a nice touch of luxury; along with the mussels, they add their own unique quality.

My fish stew

Serves 8

1 monkfish tail, about 1.5kg, bone removed and reserved, trimmed of sinews
2 gurnard, 600g each, filleted (heads and bones reserved)
8 large or 16 medium scallops, shelled and cleaned
40 live mussels, de-bearded and rinsed (see page 99)
1 garlic clove, peeled and chopped
1 rosemary sprig, leaves picked and chopped
Zest of 1 lemon (microplaned)
100ml light olive oil
1 large cod head, cleaned
300ml white wine
Sea salt and freshly ground black pepper

For the stew

2 onions, peeled and sliced
4 garlic cloves, peeled and crushed
2 fennel bulbs, finely chopped
2 red peppers, cored, deseeded and sliced
½ tsp dried chilli flakes
Zest and juice of ½ orange (zest microplaned)
A big pinch of saffron strands
3 bay leaves
1 rosemary sprig
50g tomato purée
8 ripe tomatoes, chopped

To serve

1 large baguette
Light rapeseed oil for frying
1 garlic clove, halved
Spicy anchovy mayonnaise (see page 219)

Preheat your oven to 180°C/Fan 165°C/Gas 4.

Cut the monkfish into 8 equal chunks. Halve each gurnard fillet to give 8 pieces. Put the monkfish, gurnard, scallops and mussels into a bowl and add the garlic, rosemary, lemon zest, olive oil and some salt and pepper. Mix carefully, cover and leave to marinate in the fridge for 1 hour.

To make the stock, line a roasting tray with a sheet of baking parchment. Lay the cod head and reserved fish heads and bones on the paper and roast for 25 minutes. Turn them over and roast for another 25 minutes.

Place the tray over a medium heat on the hob. Add the wine, stirring and scraping to deglaze. Simmer for 5 minutes, then tip everything into a big cooking pot and add water to cover. Bring to the boil and skim off any impurities from the surface. Lower the heat and simmer for 30 minutes.

Meanwhile, heat another large pan over a medium heat and add a drizzle of olive oil. When it is hot, add the onions, garlic, fennel and red peppers. Cook, stirring occasionally, for 5 minutes. Now add the chilli flakes, orange zest, saffron, bay and rosemary and cook for 2 minutes. Stir in the tomato purée and cook, stirring frequently, for 5 minutes.

Add the chopped tomatoes and orange juice. Cook, stirring occasionally, for 10 minutes. Pour the stock through a sieve onto the vegetables and simmer for 20 minutes. Taste and adjust the seasoning, if necessary.

In the meantime, cut the baguette into thin slices. Heat a 1cm depth of rapeseed oil in a wide pan. When hot, shallow-fry the bread slices until golden on both sides. Drain the croûtes on kitchen paper, rub with the cut surface of the garlic and season with salt.

Add the monkfish to the stew base and cook for 1 minute, then add the gurnard and mussels and cook for another 2 minutes. Finally add the scallops and cook for 1 minute.

Serve the stew in the centre of the table with the croûtes and spicy anchovy mayonnaise on the side.

Bowl food

108

This stew is very simple and quick to cook. It's a recipe that has saved me a few times when I've been really up against it. I've used beans here but potatoes also work well. You can include seasonal vegetables too, if you like – I often add squash in the autumn and asparagus during spring. Monkfish is great for this sort of dish because it can handle bold flavours and it doesn't break up on cooking. If you can't get hold of monkfish, try using gurnard, grey mullet or prawns – they all work well.

Monkfish, bean and bacon stew

Serves 4

600g monkfish fillet, trimmed
  and cut into equal chunks
A drizzle of olive oil
50g unsalted butter
2 red onions, peeled and
  chopped
2 garlic cloves, peeled and
  chopped
120g piece of smoked streaky
  bacon, cut into lardons
400g tin cannellini beans,
  drained
1 tbsp thyme leaves
1 litre fish or vegetable stock
  (see page 218)
A handful of flat-leaf parsley,
  chopped
Sea salt and freshly ground
  black pepper

Heat a large pan over a medium heat and add the olive oil and butter. When hot, add the onions and garlic and cook until the onions begin to colour. Add the bacon and cook for 5 minutes, stirring from time to time to make sure it colours evenly. No burnt bits!

Add the cannellini beans, thyme and stock and simmer for 20 minutes. Now add the monkfish and poach gently for 4 minutes. Season with salt to taste.

To finish, add the chopped parsley and stir gently. Share the stew equally between 4 warmed bowls and serve some green vegetables on the side, if you wish, and hunks of good crusty bread.

Cuttlefish is perfect for a curry, because it readily takes on the spicing and responds well to slow cooking; this is especially true of bigger cuttles. If you can't get hold of cuttlefish, or simply want a quicker curry, you can use a firm fleshed fish like monkfish or gurnard instead. I've used curry powder here for convenience, but you can grind and mix your own spices if you prefer.

Cuttlefish curry with chickpeas and spinach

Serves 4

600–800g cuttlefish, cleaned
  and cut into equal chunks
Sunflower oil for cooking
2 white onions, peeled and
  chopped
4 garlic cloves, peeled and
  chopped
2 tbsp chopped fresh ginger
2 red chillies, deseeded and
  chopped
2 tsp Madras curry powder
1 tsp garam masala
1 aubergine, peeled and diced
600g ripe tomatoes, chopped
400ml tin coconut milk
400g tin chickpeas, drained
100g baby spinach leaves
A handful of coriander, leaves
  picked
Sea salt

Heat a large sauté pan over a high heat, then add a drizzle of oil. When hot, add the cuttlefish chunks and fry for 3 minutes, turning as necessary to colour evenly. Transfer the cuttlefish to a colander set over a bowl.

Place the pan back over a medium heat and add another drizzle of oil. When hot, add the onions, garlic, ginger and chillies. Fry for 5 minutes until the onions are softened and starting to brown. Stir in the curry powder and garam masala and cook for another 2 minutes.

Now add the aubergine and tomatoes and cook for another 5 minutes until the vegetables begin to collapse. Give the curry base a really good stir and then return the cuttlefish to the pan. Pour in the coconut milk and top up with enough water to just cover everything. Bring to the boil and add a good pinch of salt.

Turn the heat down so that the curry is simmering very gently and cook for 1½ hours, topping up the liquor with more water if necessary to ensure everything remains covered.

When the cuttlefish is soft and cooked, add the chickpeas and cook for a further 15 minutes, but don't add any more water now – you want the liquor to reduce and thicken.

Add the spinach and coriander, then taste for seasoning, adding more salt if required.

Share the curry equally between 4 warmed bowls and serve with yoghurt and rice if you like. I prefer to eat it on its own with naan bread to mop up the sauce.

Bowl food

This recipe is dedicated to Joseph Tyers, a truly gifted chef who is sadly no longer with us. Joe's parents found it in the collection of recipes he wrote and told me it was one of his favourites. I didn't have the opportunity to taste the kedgeree cooked by Joe, but I've since made it several times and it's always well received. So this is Joe's recipe, not mine. I hope you enjoy it... we all have.

Joe's kedgeree

Serves 4

400g smoked haddock, skinned
300g long-grain rice
4 medium or large eggs
A splash of sunflower oil
50g unsalted butter
2 shallots, peeled and finely chopped
1 leek (white part only), well washed and finely sliced
1 celery stick (de-stringed (with a peeler) and finely sliced
1 garlic clove, peeled and finely chopped
A pinch of saffron strands
½ tsp curry powder
700ml fish stock (see page 218)
2 tsp chopped coriander leaves
Sea salt and freshly ground black pepper
1 lemon, cut into wedges, to serve

Preheat your oven to 200°C/Fan 185°C/Gas 6. Check the smoked haddock for any pin-bones and cut it into 2cm squares; set aside.

Wash the rice in cold water 4 or 5 times, changing the water each time. Drain and allow to stand in the colander for 15 minutes.

Add the eggs to a pan of simmering salted water, return to a simmer and cook for 8–10 minutes. Drain and briefly run under cold water to cool, then peel and slice.

Place a large ovenproof sauté pan over a medium heat and add the oil and butter. When hot, add the shallots, leek, celery and garlic and cook for 2 minutes without colouring.

Add the rice to the pan, stir and cook for 1 minute. Now add the saffron and curry powder and stir well over the heat.

Pour in the fish stock and bring to a simmer. Put the lid on and place the pan in the oven for 15 minutes or until the rice is cooked.

Remove from the oven, stir through the pieces of smoked haddock and immediately put the lid back on. Leave to stand for 3–5 minutes; the fish will cook in the residual heat.

Remove the lid and carefully fold through the sliced boiled eggs and coriander. Season with salt and pepper to taste. Serve the kedgeree in warmed bowls, with lemon wedges on the side.

This is a really heart-warming winter bowl of food. Ox cheeks have a great flavour and become meltingly tender if you cook them right. Here they make a brilliant partner for meaty cod cheeks. Both can handle beer quite well, so the marriage is a happy (cheeky!) one. Monkfish cheeks work equally well here, if you happen to come across them. I like to serve this with a swede, carrot and horseradish mash.

Cod and ox cheek stew

Serves 4

500g cod cheeks, trimmed of sinews
2 ox cheeks, trimmed of sinews
75ml olive oil
2 tbsp plain flour
100g piece of smoked streaky bacon, cut into lardons
4 shallots, peeled and chopped
6 garlic cloves, peeled and chopped
2 rosemary sprigs, leaves picked and chopped
4 tbsp tomato purée
6 ripe plum tomatoes, chopped
100ml red wine vinegar
500ml IPA beer
4 carrots, peeled and halved lengthways
4 tsp chopped parsley
Grated zest of 1 lemon
Sea salt and freshly ground black pepper

Preheat your oven to 140°C/Fan 125°C/Gas 1.

To cook the ox cheeks, heat a heavy-based ovenproof sauté pan over a medium-high heat, then add 3 tbsp of the olive oil. Dust the ox cheeks with the flour, seasoned with salt and pepper. Add the ox cheeks to the pan and fry for 4 minutes, turning as necessary to colour evenly all over. Using a slotted spoon, remove the ox cheeks to a plate.

Add the remaining olive oil to the pan, followed by the bacon, shallots, garlic and rosemary. Sweat over a medium heat for 3–4 minutes, then add the tomato purée and cook for a further 4 minutes. Add the chopped tomatoes and cook for another 5 minutes, stirring occasionally.

Return the ox cheeks to the pan and add the wine vinegar and beer. Bring to a simmer, then top up the liquor with enough water to cover the ox cheeks. Bring back to a simmer, put the lid on and transfer the pan to the oven. Cook slowly for 4 hours. To check that the ox cheeks are done, lift the lid and pierce one with a knife; it should pass through easily. If there is some resistance, they will need a bit longer in the oven.

In the meantime, steam or boil the carrots until just tender.

Once the ox cheeks are cooked, transfer the pan back to the hob. Add the cod cheeks to the stew, along with the carrots. Return to a simmer and poach gently for 3–4 minutes.

To serve, share the stew equally between 4 warmed bowls. Finish with a sprinkling of chopped parsley and grated lemon zest. Serve with mash.

Bowl food   115

Octopus goes down really well with my customers. It's definitely one of those things they eat when they are out because they think it's hard to get right at home. Nonsense, octopus is really simple to do! Follow my recipe and you will wonder why you haven't tried it before. The lovely Spanish romesco sauce works really well with the caramelised octopus.

Braised octopus with romesco sauce

Serves 4

1 octopus (double sucker species), about 1kg (defrosted if frozen)
Olive oil for cooking
1 onion, peeled and chopped
4 garlic cloves, peeled and chopped
3 bay leaves
3 tsp sweet smoked paprika
Sea salt and freshly ground black pepper

For the romesco sauce

20g crustless white bread
3 tbsp olive oil
3 red peppers, quartered, cored and deseeded
200g ripe plum tomatoes, halved
30g blanched almonds
30g skinned hazelnuts
2 garlic cloves, peeled and chopped
2 tbsp sherry vinegar
400g tin cannellini beans
1 bunch of spring onions, sliced

To serve

Sweet smoked paprika to sprinkle

Heat a pan large enough to hold the octopus and add a generous drizzle of olive oil. When hot, add the onion, garlic, bay leaves and smoked paprika and cook for 2 minutes. Add the whole octopus and some salt and pepper. Put the lid on and cook for 1 hour, or until the octopus is tender. To check, insert a knife into a tentacle; it should cut through with ease. If not, continue to cook, checking every 10 minutes until it is ready.

Meanwhile, make the sauce. Preheat your grill to high. Blitz the bread in a blender to crumbs. Oil and season the peppers and tomatoes all over, then lay skin side up on a large grill tray. Grill until the skins are blistered and blackened. Peel away the skins when cool enough to handle.

Place a frying pan over a medium heat and add a drizzle of olive oil. When it is hot, add the nuts and fry, stirring occasionally, until golden all over. Tip out onto a plate and leave to cool. Heat a little more oil in the pan and fry the breadcrumbs and garlic until golden and crisp.

Tip the garlicky crumbs into a blender, add the tomatoes, peppers and nuts and pulse to a rough paste. Add the sherry vinegar with some salt and pepper and blend for 10 seconds. Transfer to a bowl and set aside.

When the octopus is cooked, lift it out on a tray and leave until cool enough to handle. Reserve the stock. Cut off and reserve the tentacles. Slit open the main body and remove the ink sac, stomach and eyes carefully. Chop all the main body meat up and put to one side.

When ready to serve, in a large pan, mix the cooled, chopped octopus body meat into the sauce. Add the beans, spring onions and 200ml of the octopus stock (or more if you prefer a 'soupy' dish). Heat through.

Meanwhile, place a frying pan over a high heat. Oil and season the tentacles. When the pan is hot, add a little oil, then the tentacles. Cook for 2 minutes on each side until nicely coloured and lightly charred.

Season the stew and share between 4 bowls. Slice the tentacles and share between the bowls. Sprinkle generously with smoked paprika and serve.

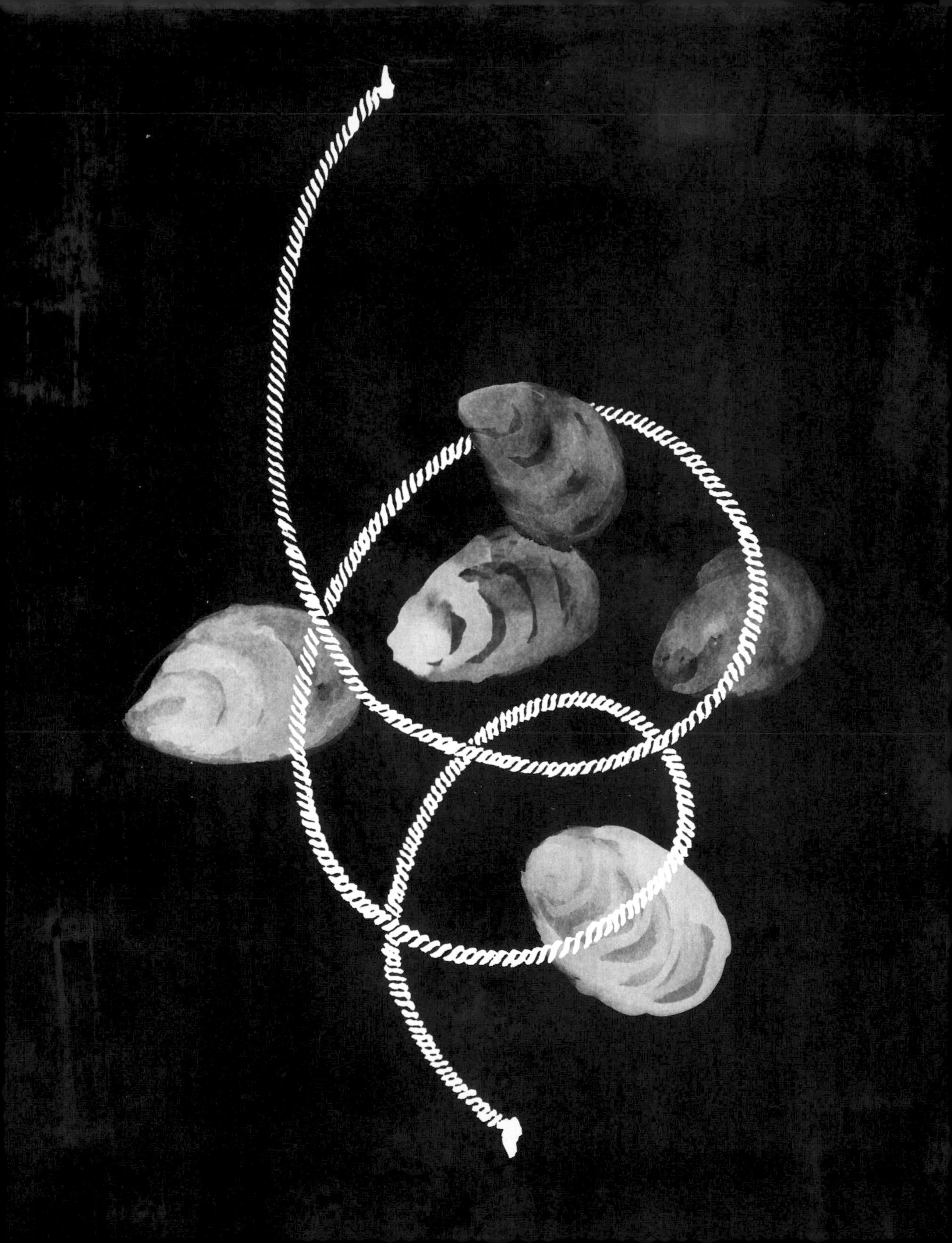

SEAFOOD SALADS

I love the texture of octopus, when it is cooked perfectly. In this salad the char from grilling it, combined with the smooth softness of the avocado, adds to the excitement. The double sucker species of octopus is the best one to use, as it cooks really well. Most of the time, octopus comes frozen but that's not a bad thing. In fact, the freezing process helps to tenderise the meat. You could also make this salad with squid or cuttlefish.

Octopus, avocado and tomato salad, lime and coriander dressing

Serves 4 as a starter or light lunch

1 octopus (double sucker species), about 1kg (defrosted if frozen)
Olive oil for cooking
1 white onion, peeled and roughly chopped
4 garlic cloves, peeled and crushed
2 rosemary sprigs
Finely grated zest and juice of 1 lime
100ml white wine
Sea salt and freshly ground black pepper

For the salad

2 ripe avocados
20 cherry or baby plum tomatoes, halved
100g rocket leaves

For the lime and coriander dressing

150ml extra virgin olive oil
Zest and juice of 1 lime
1 tbsp Dijon mustard
2 tbsp chopped coriander

Heat a pan large enough to hold the octopus and add a drizzle of olive oil. When hot, add the onion, garlic, rosemary and lime zest. Sweat for 3 minutes, then add the octopus, wine and lime juice. Put the lid on the pan and simmer gently for 1 hour or until the octopus is tender. To check, insert a knife into one of the tentacles; it should cut through with ease. If not, continue to cook, checking every 10 minutes until it is ready.

When the octopus is cooked, lift it out on a tray and leave until cool enough to handle. Cut off and reserve the tentacles. Slit open the main body and remove the ink sac, stomach and eyes carefully. Cut the meat into strips, thread onto a skewer and put to one side.

Heat up a chargrill or barbecue. Meanwhile, halve, stone and peel the avocados, then cut into slices and place in a bowl with the tomatoes and mix gently.

Oil the octopus pieces and tentacles and season with salt and pepper. Place both the skewered meat and tentacles on the chargrill or barbecue and cook for 5–6 minutes until the outside is caramelised and golden.

Meanwhile, to make the dressing, whisk the ingredients together in a bowl and season with salt and pepper to taste.

Remove the octopus from the skewers and add to the tomato and avocado with the tentacles. Add a few spoonfuls of dressing and toss gently, then add the rocket leaves and a pinch of salt. Share the salad equally between 4 plates and finish with another drizzle of dressing.

Seafood salads

Squid is a crowd pleaser for sure! Crumbed or battered and deep-fried, it always flies off any menu, but to me it has so much more to offer. For this salad I have quickly poached small squid and lightly pickled them before tossing with shaved cauliflower, spicy salami and peppery watercress. It can be served cold, warm or hot – the choice is yours.

Squid, watercress and cauliflower salad with salami

Serves 4 as a starter or light lunch

600g small squid, cleaned, body cut into rings, fins scored
2 garlic cloves, peeled and chopped
1 small cauliflower, finely sliced (ideally on a mandoline)
A bunch of watercress, leaves picked
150g spicy salami, sliced and cut into strips

For the dressing

150ml extra virgin olive oil
75ml white wine vinegar
1 red onion, peeled and finely sliced
Sea salt and freshly ground black pepper

For the dressing, whisk the olive oil and wine vinegar together in a large bowl, then add the red onion and some salt and pepper. Set aside.

In a saucepan, bring around 1 litre of water to the boil and season generously with salt. Add the garlic and simmer for 2 minutes. Add the squid to the water and blanch for 30 seconds, then remove and drain well. Drop the squid straight into the dressing and mix together. Leave to cool.

When ready to serve, add the cauliflower and watercress to the squid mixture along with the salami. Toss to combine and season with salt and pepper to taste. Serve immediately.

This is a perfect, simple salad for a summer's day, especially when tomatoes are plentiful, juicy and sweet. It's always nice to cook your own crab, but if you can get hold of a good one, freshly picked, you can assemble the salad in next to no time. The horseradish adds a refreshing hot kick and really brings the salad alive.

Crab and tomato salad with horseradish dressing

Serves 4 as a starter

About 300g white crabmeat (from a 1.5kg freshly cooked crab)
12 ripe tomatoes (the best variety you can get)
1 shallot, peeled and finely chopped
100ml olive oil
50ml white wine vinegar
1 tsp caster sugar
3 tsp chopped parsley
Sea salt and freshly ground black pepper

For the horseradish dressing

150ml soured cream
2 tbsp creamed horseradish
Finely grated zest and juice of 1 lemon
100g brown crabmeat, sieved

To garnish

Zest of 1 lemon (microplaned)
2 tbsp flat-leaf parsley leaves, sliced

Bring a pan of water (large enough to hold all the tomatoes) to the boil. Remove the cores from the tomatoes and score a cross in the skin on the top of each one. Lower the tomatoes into the boiling water and blanch for 20 seconds, then remove to a tray. When cool enough to handle, peel off the skins. Cut half of the tomatoes into slices the thickness of a £1 coin; cut the rest into wedges.

Place all the tomatoes in a bowl and add the shallot, olive oil, wine vinegar, sugar and chopped parsley. Toss gently to mix and season with salt and pepper to taste. Set aside.

Check through the white crabmeat carefully for fragments of shell or cartilage. Place the crabmeat in a bowl and season with salt and pepper.

For the dressing, whisk the ingredients together in a bowl until smoothly combined. Season with salt and pepper to taste.

To serve, divide the tomato salad between 4 plates. Share the white crabmeat equally between the plates and drizzle the dressing over the salad. Finish with a sprinkling of lemon zest and parsley.

Seafood salads

Potatoes, chilli and prawns sit so well together in this effortless, comforting salad. I like to eat it just as it is, but you could serve it as a side salad if you like. I have also made it with crab, lobster and scallops – all work brilliantly. I make it quite spicy, so if you don't like the heat, you might want to cut down on the chilli. It is really versatile and can be served hot, warm or cold. I love it!

Prawn, chilli and potato salad

Serves 4 as a starter or light lunch

600g large raw prawns, peeled and deveined
400g small new potatoes
Sunflower oil for cooking
4 spring onions, trimmed and sliced
2 tbsp finely sliced coriander, plus extra leaves to serve
1 tbsp finely sliced mint, plus extra leaves to serve
Sea salt and freshly ground black pepper

For the sauce
Sunflower oil for cooking
1 red onion, peeled and finely chopped
3 garlic cloves, peeled, halved (germ removed) and chopped
2 red chillies, deseeded and chopped
1 tsp black onion seeds
1 tsp coriander seeds
4 ripe tomatoes, core removed, deseeded and chopped
Sea salt and freshly ground black pepper

First make the sauce. Heat a frying pan over a medium heat and add a drizzle of sunflower oil. When it is hot, add the onion, garlic, chillies and spices and fry for 3–4 minutes until the mixture begins to colour. Add the chopped tomatoes, season with salt and pepper and cook for 6–8 minutes until they begin to collapse.

Transfer the contents of the pan to a food processor and blend until the mixture is as smooth as you can get it. Pass through a sieve into a clean bowl and allow to cool.

Add the prawns to the cooled sauce and leave to marinate for at least 10 minutes, longer if you have the time.

To cook the new potatoes, put them into a pan, cover with water and add a pinch of salt. Bring to the boil, then lower the heat and simmer for 10–15 minutes until they are cooked. Drain thoroughly and leave to cool slightly while you cook the prawns.

Heat a frying pan over a high heat. Remove the prawns from the sauce with a slotted spoon, keeping the sauce. Add a drizzle of oil to the hot pan, then carefully add the prawns and cook for 2 minutes on each side.

Add the sauce to the pan and bring to a simmer, then take off the heat. Stir in the spring onions, coriander and mint. Now add the potatoes (or combine in a bowl if your pan is too small). Season the prawn salad with salt and pepper to taste and toss well.

Serve the salad scatted with extra coriander and mint leaves, either on its own, or with a green salad if you prefer.

Seafood salads

Sometimes, perfectly cooked simple seafood and good mayonnaise is all you need to impress. If you are entertaining, this is often the best way to go, as everything can be done in advance. Remember to remove this dish from the fridge half an hour or so before serving to take the chill off the lobsters. Verjus gives seafood a lovely fresh acidity.

Dressed lobster with herb mayonnaise

Serves 2 as a light lunch

2 live lobsters, up to 1kg each
2 shallots, peeled and sliced
1 fennel bulb, trimmed and
  sliced
2 carrots, peeled and sliced
2 garlic cloves, peeled and
  crushed
2 thyme sprigs
2 bay leaves
10 black peppercorns
200ml verjus
Olive oil to drizzle
Salt

For the herb mayonnaise

2 egg yolks
1 tsp English mustard
1 small garlic clove, peeled
  and chopped
1 shallot, peeled and finely
  chopped
1½ tbsp verjus
200ml light olive oil
1 tbsp chopped chives
1 tbsp chopped tarragon
Sea salt

Put the lobsters in the freezer for an hour before cooking to sedate them.

To cook the lobsters, put the vegetables, garlic, herbs, peppercorns and verjus into a large pan (big enough to hold all the lobsters). Pour in enough water to cover the lobsters and add plenty of salt. Bring to the boil over a high heat, then lower the heat and simmer for 5 minutes.

In the meantime, take the lobsters out of the freezer and firmly insert the tip of a strong cook's knife into the cross on the head to kill each one instantly. Add the lobsters to the simmering bouillon and cook for 6 minutes, then remove the pan from the heat.

Leave the lobsters in the bouillon for 2 minutes to finish cooking in the residual heat, then lift them out. Strain the bouillon and let it cool. Place the lobsters on a tray and leave to cool completely.

Meanwhile, make the mayonnaise. Put the egg yolks, mustard, garlic, shallot and verjus into a bowl and whisk together for 1 minute. Add the olive oil in a thin, steady steam, whisking as you do so, until it is all incorporated. Season with salt to taste, cover and place in the fridge.

When the lobsters are cold, carefully cut them in half lengthways, from head to tail. Remove the stomach sac from the head and the dark intestinal thread that runs along the length of the tail. Crack the claws and knuckles and lay the lobsters on a large platter.

When ready to serve, mix the chopped herbs into the mayonnaise and spoon some into the head part of the shell. Drizzle the lobsters with a little bouillon and olive oil. Serve at once, with the rest of the mayonnaise in a bowl on the side.

Seafood salads

This lovely, summery dish is really quick to knock up. Red mullet is such a treat and the aubergine and basil go perfectly – to give the dish a Mediterranean feel. You can also turn this into a really great pasta meal. Just boil some linguine and pan-fry the fish, then add the salad and dressing and toss the whole lot together. I've done that at home too and everyone liked it.

Red mullet and aubergine salad with basil dressing

Serves 4 as a starter or light lunch

4 red mullet, 300–400g each, scaled, gutted and butterfly filleted
Olive oil for cooking
Sea salt and freshly ground black pepper

For the aubergine salad
75ml olive oil
2 red onions, peeled and sliced
2 aubergines, peeled and diced
75ml balsamic vinegar
2 handfuls of rocket leaves
2 tbsp pine nuts
100g green olives, pitted and sliced
A little extra virgin olive oil to dress

For the basil dressing
1 shallot, peeled and finely sliced
1 garlic clove, peeled, halved (germ removed) and finely chopped
4 anchovy fillets in oil, drained and finely chopped
50g green olives, pitted and chopped
A bunch of basil, picked
150ml olive oil
75ml white wine vinegar

First make the dressing. Put the shallot, garlic, anchovies and olives in a food processor and blitz for 1 minute. Add the basil and blitz for another minute, then scrape down the sides of the bowl. Now, with the motor running, pour in the olive oil in a thin, steady stream through the funnel. Finally, add the wine vinegar and season to taste with salt and pepper. Set aside.

For the salad, heat a large pan (that has a tight-fitting lid) over a medium heat and add the olive oil. When it is hot, add the red onions and cook for 5 minutes until they start to soften. Next, add the aubergines and give the mixture a good stir. Cover and cook for 5 minutes, stirring a couple of times.

Add the balsamic vinegar and cook, uncovered, for another 3 minutes, or until the aubergine is cooked. Spoon the mixture onto a tray and allow to cool.

Preheat the grill to cook the fish. Lay the butterflied red mullet fillets skin side up on an oiled grill tray and season all over with salt and pepper. Place the fillets under the grill and cook for 4 minutes.

While the fish is cooking, tip the aubergine mixture into a bowl and add the rocket, pine nuts and olives. Toss to mix and season the salad with salt and pepper. Dress with a drizzle of good olive oil.

Share the salad between 4 plates. When cooked, lay a butterflied red mullet on top of each portion and drizzle the basil dressing around the plates. Serve straight away.

I generally use very good quality farmed salmon for this dish, rather than wild salmon, which is something of a delicacy these days. Kohlrabi lends a nice crunchy texture and earthy freshness to the salad and makes it more of a wintry dish. If you wanted to serve it as a summer salad, you could replace the kohlrabi with refreshing cucumber or ripe tomatoes.

Salmon and kohlrabi tartare salad

Serves 6–8 as a starter or light lunch

1 side of good quality farmed or wild salmon, pin-boned

For the court bouillon

3 shallots, peeled and sliced
2 carrots, peeled and sliced
2 bay leaves
A few thyme sprigs
45g sea salt
150ml verjus
A handful of parsley
2 litres water
1 tsp black peppercorns

For the kohlrabi tartare salad

1 red onion, peeled and finely sliced
50ml verjus
2 kohlrabi, peeled, halved and finely sliced (ideally on a mandoline)
1 tbsp capers in brine, rinsed
2 large gherkins, thinly sliced
1 tbsp each chopped curly parsley, tarragon, chervil and chives
75ml cold-pressed rapeseed oil
Sea salt and freshly ground black pepper

For the salad cream

2 egg yolks
2 tsp English mustard
2 tsp caster sugar
2 tbsp verjus
100ml cold-pressed rapeseed oil
1 tbsp each chopped curly parsley, tarragon, chervil and chives
150ml double cream

To make the court bouillon for poaching the salmon, put the shallots, carrots, bay leaves, thyme, salt, verjus and parsley into a pan and cover with the water. Bring to the boil, skim off any impurities and simmer for 15 minutes. Add the peppercorns and remove from the heat.

For the salad, put the red onion into a large bowl, add the verjus and set aside for 10 minutes or so to mingle and soften.

Preheat your oven to 200°C/Fan 185°C/Gas 6.

To make the salad cream, put the egg yolks, mustard, sugar and verjus into a bowl and whisk for 1 minute, then gradually whisk in the oil, drop by drop to begin with until you have an emulsion, then add the rest in a thin stream. To finish, whisk in the herbs and cream and season with salt and pepper to taste. Cover and refrigerate until ready to serve.

Bring the court bouillon back to a simmer. Meanwhile, for the salad, add the sliced kohlrabi to the red onion, followed by the capers, gherkins and herbs. Toss well and season with salt and pepper to taste.

Cut the salmon in half to fit in a deep roasting tray. Line the tray with baking parchment or silicone paper and lay the salmon on top. Pour the contents of the court bouillon pan over the salmon and place in the oven. Cook for 12–14 minutes, then carefully remove the tray from the oven and lift the salmon onto a plate to cool. When cool enough to handle, flake the salmon into nice chunks.

To serve, spoon three-quarters of the kohlrabi onto a large platter, then add the chunks of poached salmon. Add the remaining salad, spoon on the salad cream and serve.

I love the freshness and textures of this salad: the tender courgettes, crunchy nuts, zingy dressing and oily goodness of the fish. The sardines need to be spanking fresh, but if you can't get hold of any really fresh sardines, then mackerel, sprats or herring will work. Failing that, I have made this recipe with really good quality tinned sardines.

Sardines with courgette and nut salad

Serves 4 as a starter or light lunch

8 sardines, scaled, gutted and
  butterfly filleted
Olive oil for cooking
Finely grated zest of 1 lemon
Sea salt and freshly ground
  black pepper

**For the courgette and
nut salad**

1 red onion, peeled and finely
  sliced
3 large courgettes
50g roasted peanuts, chopped
50g roasted cashews,
  chopped
50g pine nuts, toasted
2 tbsp chopped dill

For the lemon dressing

100ml olive oil
Finely grated zest and juice
  of 1 lemon
100ml groundnut oil

Preheat your grill to its highest setting.

For the dressing, whisk the olive oil, lemon zest and juice, and the oil together in a bowl and season with salt and pepper to taste.

Add the red onion to the dressing and leave to stand for 10 minutes; this will take the raw edge off the taste.

Meanwhile, using a mandoline if you have one, cut the courgettes into matchsticks and place in a bowl. Remove the red onion from the dressing with a slotted spoon and add to the courgettes with 6 tbsp of the dressing; mix well. Set aside. Reserve the rest of the dressing.

To cook the sardines, lay the butterflied fillets skin side down on an oiled grill tray. Season the flesh side with salt and pepper and sprinkle with the lemon zest, then turn the fillets over. Place the tray under the grill and cook the fillets skin side up for about 4 minutes until they are cooked through, then remove from the tray.

Add the cooking juices from the grill tray to the courgettes and toss to combine. Add the nuts and chopped dill, mix gently, then share the salad equally between 4 warmed plates. Lay the butterflied sardines on top and drizzle with the rest of the dressing.

Seafood salads

Seafood salads

I adore mackerel and my favourite food to eat out is Asian, so I was keen to bring the two together. I created this salad for a party at home from the Asian ingredients I had in my kitchen cupboards. The texture of the mackerel and its natural oiliness work beautifully with the Asian flavourings. Saying that, you could put any oily fish with this dish – sardines would be a fantastic alternative.

Mackerel and noodle salad, cashew and lime dressing

Serves 4

4 mackerel, filleted, trimmed and pin-boned
1 litre sunflower oil, for deep-frying
3 banana shallots, peeled and finely sliced, separated into rings
100g plain flour
100g cashew nuts
Sea salt

For the noodle salad

300g dried noodles
2 large carrots, peeled and cut into fine julienne
4 spring onions, finely sliced
50g fresh ginger, grated
4 garlic cloves, peeled and grated
A bunch of radishes, finely sliced
A handful of mint leaves, roughly chopped
A handful of coriander leaves

For the cashew and lime dressing

100ml fish sauce
Finely grated zest and juice of 2 limes
75g palm sugar or soft brown sugar
1 shallot, peeled and finely chopped
2 garlic cloves, peeled and grated
1 red chilli, halved, deseeded and sliced

Heat the oil for deep-frying in a deep, heavy pan to 170°C. Toss the shallot rings through the flour seasoned with salt, shaking off any excess (save for the mackerel). Fry the shallot rings in the hot oil until golden and crisp. Remove with a slotted spoon and drain on kitchen paper. Season the shallots with salt and set aside to cool.

Next, fry the cashews in the oil for 2–3 minutes until golden. Lift out of with a slotted spoon and drain on kitchen paper. Season with salt and put to one side.

Pass the mackerel through the flour and knock off any excess. Fry 4 fillets at a time for 3 minutes. Remove and drain on kitchen paper. Season with salt and leave to cool.

For the salad, bring a pan of water to the boil, add salt, then drop in the noodles and take off the heat. Leave to soften for 3 minutes, then drain the noodles well in a colander (excess water will dilute the dressing).

Heat a large frying pan or wok and add a drizzle of the oil from the fish pan. When hot, add the carrots, spring onions, ginger and garlic. Stir-fry for 2 minutes until the veg start to soften. Remove and set aside.

To make the dressing, put the fish sauce, lime juice and sugar into a pan over a medium heat until the sugar is dissolved. Take off the heat and add the shallot, garlic, chilli and lime zest.

To assemble, put the noodles, stir-fried veg and dressing into a large bowl and toss well. Add the radishes, mint and most of the coriander and toss again. Taste for seasoning, and add a little more salt if required. Arrange on a large platter or divide between 4 bowls.

Break the mackerel into chunks and place on top of the salad. Finally, scatter over the fried cashews, shallots and remaining coriander leaves. Serve at room temperature or warm.

Seafood salads

If you see John Dory on the fishmonger's block, buy it. It's a great fish with a delicate texture and delicious sweet flavour, but it's not always available. I like to serve this salad as a springtime lunch dish. The zesty flavours will brighten up your day.

John Dory, shaved asparagus, chilli and orange salad

Serves 4

4 John Dory, about 500g
  each, gutted, filleted and
  skinned
2 red onions, peeled
16 asparagus spears, woody
  parts removed
4 red chillies, halved,
  deseeded and thinly sliced
1 orange
Sea salt and freshly ground
  black pepper

For the dressing
4 tbsp verjus
4 tbsp olive oil
1 tbsp Dijon mustard
1 tbsp honey
2 tbsp coriander leaves,
  chopped
2 tbsp mint leaves, chopped

Preheat the grill to high, ready to cook the fish.

Using a mandoline if you have one, slice the red onions and asparagus as thinly as possible and place in a large bowl with the sliced chillies. Finely grate the zest of the orange and add to the salad. Cut away the peel and pith from the orange and cut out the segments from between the membranes; add to the salad and toss to combine.

For the dressing, whisk the ingredients together in a bowl and season with salt and pepper.

Add half of the dressing to the asparagus salad and toss lightly. Taste and add more seasoning if required.

Season the fish all over with salt and pepper, then lay on the grill tray. Place under the grill for 3 minutes, then turn the fillets over and cook the other side for 3 minutes.

To serve, share most of the asparagus salad between 4 warmed plates. Place a grilled fish fillet on top, arrange the remaining salad on the fish and drizzle over the reserved dressing. Serve immediately.

Seafood salads

As soon as parsnips are at their best, you've just got to try this warm, autumnal salad. The cod and bacon flavours work really well with parsnip and kale. I like to flake the grilled cod through the salad but you could leave it as a whole fillet if you prefer. The salad is also delicious with carrots in place of the parsnips.

Cod, bacon, kale and parsnip salad

Serves 4

600g cod fillet, skinned and
   pin-boned
2 large parsnips
Olive oil for cooking and
   to dress
1 garlic clove, peeled and
   roughly chopped
75g butter
200g kale, stalks removed
6 rashers of smoked streaky
   bacon
4 tsp chopped parsley
Finely grated zest and juice
   of 1 lemon
Sea salt and freshly ground
   black pepper

Peel the parsnips and slice each one lengthways into 8 ribbons. Place a large frying pan over a medium heat and add a drizzle of olive oil. When hot, add the garlic and parsnips and cook for 2–3 minutes until the parsnips start to colour. Now add the butter and some salt and pepper. Cook for another 5–6 minutes until the parsnips are golden and starting to soften. Remove the parsnips and garlic to a tray lined with kitchen paper to drain; keep warm.

Preheat your grill to its highest setting, ready to cook the fish.

Wipe out the frying pan, put it back over a medium-high heat and add another drizzle of olive oil. When the oil is hot, add the kale and stir-fry for 3–4 minutes until it is cooked but still retains some bite. Transfer to the same tray as the parsnips; keep warm.

Place the bacon rashers and cod fillets on a well oiled grill tray. Season the fish with salt and pepper and put the tray under the grill. Cook the cod fillets for 3 minutes, then turn them over and cook for a further 2 minutes. Remove the fish as soon as it is cooked and the bacon when it is well coloured and cooked.

Chop the bacon and place it in a large bowl. Chop the kale and add it to the bowl. Next flake the cod and add it too. Finally, add the parsnips, garlic, parsley, lemon zest and juice, and a drizzle of olive oil. Season the salad with salt and pepper to taste, then carefully toss it all together.

Share the salad between 4 warmed plates and serve straight away.

Smoked fish and pickles work so well together. The acidity of the pickle cuts the richness of the fish with every mouthful, to delicious effect. If you prepare the pickled veg in advance you can assemble this salad in 5 minutes – perfect for a quick lunch. If you're feeling like showing off though, you can top the salad with some freshly grilled mackerel fillets.

Smoked mackerel and pickled vegetable salad

Serves 4

6 smoked mackerel fillets
2 tsp creamed horseradish
Finely grated zest and juice
 of 1 lime

**For the pickled vegetable
 salad**
100ml cider
100ml cider vinegar
100ml water
100g caster sugar
1 banana shallot, peeled and
 sliced into rings
1 carrot, peeled and thinly
 sliced
1 fennel bulb, tough outer
 layer removed, shredded
 (ideally on a mandoline)
1 celery stick, de-stringed
 (with a peeler) and finely
 sliced
1 red pepper, peeled, cored,
 deseeded and finely sliced
1 garlic clove, peeled and
 crushed
Sea salt and freshly ground
 black pepper

To serve
Cold-pressed rapeseed oil
 to drizzle
Mustard and cress or salad
 leaves

For the pickled vegetables, put the cider, cider vinegar, water and sugar into a pan over a medium heat to dissolve the sugar. Put all the prepared vegetables and garlic into a bowl large enough to hold them and the pickling liquor. Bring the pickling liquor to the boil, then pour over the vegetables. Cover the bowl with a disc of greaseproof paper, pushing it down so that it keeps all the vegetables submerged, and set aside to cool.

To prepare the fish, remove the skin and cut down the middle of the fillet to cut out all the little bones. Flake the fish into a bowl and mix in the horseradish, lime zest and juice.

Drain the pickled vegetables, keeping the liquor to store any leftovers.

Gently toss the pickled vegetables with the mackerel, adding a drizzle of rapeseed oil. Taste for seasoning, adding salt and/or pepper if need be.

To serve, share the salad equally between 4 plates and finish with a drizzle of rapeseed oil and cress or salad leaves.

BAKE

Cooking for a crowd is always a bit daunting, even for me! This prawn dish looks, smells and tastes amazing and is really simple to cook for a lot of people, providing you have the space. Try and find good quality sustainable prawns – it will make all the difference, trust me.

Salt and seaweed baked prawns, tomato and coriander salad

Serves 6

30 large raw prawns, peeled
  and deveined, but heads and
  tails left on
Olive oil to drizzle
2 good handfuls of dried
  seaweed
About 500g rock salt for
  baking

**For the tomato and
coriander salad**

20 ripe plum tomatoes, halved
1 bunch of spring onions,
  trimmed and sliced
75ml white wine vinegar
100ml olive oil
1 tsp ground coriander
½ tsp cayenne pepper
A handful of coriander, leaves
  picked and chopped
Sea salt and freshly ground
  black pepper

Preheat your oven to 200°C/Fan 185°C/Gas 6.

For the salad, put the tomatoes, spring onions, wine vinegar and olive oil into a bowl. Season with the ground coriander, cayenne and some salt and black pepper. Toss to mix and set aside.

Toss the prawns in a bowl with a little salt and a drizzle of olive oil.

Scatter the seaweed and rock salt in a large roasting tray. Lay the prawns on top and bake for 5 minutes, depending on the size of your prawns.

Meanwhile, add the coriander to the salad and toss together.

Remove the tray of prawns from the oven and place on a mat on the table. Eat straight away, using your hands. No time for cutlery, but provide bowls and forks for the salad, and finger bowls.

I'm particularly fond of baked scallops. Like many of my recipes, I came up with this one at home, after rummaging through the cupboards to see what I could find. Cooking the scallops in this way protects the delicate meat from direct heat, giving you a lovely soft cooked texture. Feel free to vary the flavourings for the crumbs and butter as you like.

Scallops with Cheddar crumbs, smoked paprika and coriander butter

Serves 4 as a starter

12 fresh scallops, shelled and
  cleaned (shells reserved)
240ml white wine

For the crumbs

200g crustless good quality
  bread
A handful of coriander, leaves
  picked
75g mature Cheddar, grated

**For the smoked paprika and
coriander butter**

300g unsalted butter, cut into
  cubes and softened
1 banana shallot or 2 standard
  shallots, peeled and finely
  chopped
1 garlic clove, peeled, halved
  (germ removed) and finely
  chopped
2 tsp sweet smoked paprika
A handful of coriander, leaves
  picked and finely chopped
Sea salt

To serve

1 lime, cut into wedges

Preheat your oven to 220°C/Fan 205°C/Gas 7. Clean the best 12 scallop shells, dry well and reserve for cooking.

To make the crumbs, blitz the bread and coriander in a food processor until the bread is reduced to crumbs and the coriander is finely chopped. Add the cheese and blitz for 30 seconds. Tip onto a tray and set aside.

For the butter, put the soft butter into a bowl with the shallot(s), garlic, smoked paprika and chopped coriander. Mix well to combine and season with salt to taste. Set aside until ready to cook.

When ready to eat, place one scallop in each of the reserved shells. Sprinkle 20ml white wine and dot 30g butter on each one. Scatter the crumbs evenly over the top and place the scallops on a large oven tray. (You may need to use 2 trays.)

Bake the scallops for 6–8 minutes. To check that they are cooked, insert a small knife into the centre of a scallop and hold it there for 10 seconds. Pull the knife out and place it on the back of your hand; if the blade feels hot, they are ready. (It should not be piping hot.)

Serve the scallops straight away, with lime wedges.

This is a version of the Oysters Rockefeller that we cook at Outlaw's Fish Kitchen. The Porthilly oysters we use are fantastic for cooking and great in this dish. If you have any of the flavoured butter left over, wrap it well and freeze it, but I doubt you will – it tastes too good.

Baked oysters with watercress and anise butter

Serves 4

24 live rock oysters
About 500g rock salt for
  baking
100g fresh breadcrumbs

**For the watercress and
  anise butter**
150g watercress, leaves picked
150g spinach leaves
150g unsalted butter
3 small shallots, finely
  chopped
1 small green chilli, deseeded
  and finely chopped
30ml Pastis
30g tarragon, leaves picked

To serve
Rock salt or seaweed

For the butter, bring a pan of salted water to the boil. Add the watercress and spinach and blanch for 1 minute. Immediately drain and plunge the leaves into a bowl of iced water to cool quickly. When cold, drain and squeeze out the excess water.

Heat a small pan over a medium heat and add 50g of the butter. When it is bubbling, add the shallots and chilli and sweat for 3 minutes until the shallots are translucent. Add the Pastis and simmer for 30 seconds.

Tip the contents of the pan into a blender. Let cool slightly, then add the tarragon and blanched watercress and spinach. Blitz to combine, then add the remaining 100g butter. Blend for 30 seconds, scraping down the sides of the jug once or twice. Transfer to a bowl, cover and set aside.

Preheat your oven to 200°C/Fan 185°C/Gas 6. Line a large baking tray with enough salt to allow you to sit the oyster shells on without them toppling over. Open the oysters and prise off the top shell. Drain off the juices. Cut the muscle to release the oyster but leave it in the rounded shell; check for any fragments of shell.

Top each oyster with a generous helping of the watercress butter and sprinkle with an even layer of breadcrumbs. Bake for 12 minutes, or until the breadcrumbs are golden and crispy. Serve immediately, on little salt mounds or nestled in seaweed.

This is a great way to cook those medium or slightly larger squid, which are perfect for a single portion filled with a tasty stuffing. The stuffing in this recipe isn't supposed to all stay inside the squid pouches; some of it will ooze out to create a delicious sauce. I'd suggest serving this dish with a simple rocket salad, dressed with a little balsamic vinegar and olive oil.

Stuffed squid, red peppers, chickpeas, olives and sherry

Serves 4

4 medium squid, bodies
  20–25cm long, cleaned and
  tentacles reserved
Olive oil for cooking and
  to drizzle
2 shallots, peeled and finely
  chopped
3 garlic cloves, peeled and
  finely chopped
2 red peppers, peeled, cored,
  deseeded and diced
4 ripe plum tomatoes, cored
  and each cut into 6 pieces
100g pitted black olives,
  quartered
400g tin chickpeas, drained
  and rinsed
16 basil leaves, finely sliced
500ml dry sherry
100g unsalted butter, diced
500ml fish stock (see page
  218)
Sea salt and freshly ground
  black pepper

Preheat your oven to 200°C/Fan 185°C/Gas 6.

Place a sauté pan over a medium heat and add a generous drizzle of olive oil. When hot, add the shallots, garlic and red peppers and sweat for 5 minutes. Add the tomatoes and olives and cook for a further 5 minutes until the tomatoes soften and begin to collapse. Season with salt and pepper to taste.

Add the chickpeas and cook for a further 10 minutes. Remove from the heat and allow to cool.

Lay the cleaned squid pouches in an oven tray and season all over with salt and pepper. Season the tentacles too, but set these aside on a plate.

When the stuffing mixture is cool, stir through most of the sliced basil. Now, using a spoon, fill each squid pouch with as much stuffing as it will take. If there is any stuffing mixture left, add that to the tray too.

Pour the sherry over the stuffed squid and dot with the butter. Bake for 15–20 minutes, basting with the mixture every 5 minutes. Pour on the fish stock and cook for another 10 minutes, adding the tentacles to the tray for the final 5 minutes.

Place a stuffed squid pouch on each warmed plate with the tentacles alongside and spoon on some of the sauce. Scatter over the remaining sliced basil, add a drizzle of olive oil and serve straight away.

For me, baking and steaming are the best ways to cook haddock. That's why fish and chips are so good – the fish steams inside its protective batter jacket. Other cooking techniques seem to dry out the fish too much. I'm a fan of béarnaise sauce, so I decided to create a simple butter with the same flavours. It marries so well with the fish, tomatoes and mushrooms, bringing the whole dish together. You can use cod, hake or really fresh whiting in place of the haddock, if you like.

Haddock baked in a bag with béarnaise butter

Serves 4

4 filleted haddock portions, about 150g each
8 small field mushrooms, peeled and stem removed
4 plum tomatoes, halved
Olive oil for cooking
4 garlic cloves, peeled, halved (germ removed) and finely chopped
Sea salt and freshly ground black pepper

For the béarnaise butter

250g unsalted butter, diced and softened
2 shallots, peeled and finely chopped
A handful of tarragon, leaves picked and finely chopped
1 tsp cracked black or coarsely ground black pepper
1 tsp sea salt
2 tbsp red wine vinegar

Preheat your oven to 220°C/Fan 205°C/Gas 7.

To make the béarnaise butter, put the butter, shallots, tarragon, black pepper, salt and wine vinegar into a bowl and mix until evenly combined. Taste and adjust the seasoning if necessary. Cover and set aside.

To cook the mushrooms and tomatoes, line a baking tray with two layers of foil, making sure they overlap the edges of the tray. Drizzle the top sheet of foil with olive oil and sprinkle with salt and pepper. Place the mushrooms and tomatoes on the foil and season them too. Sprinkle with the chopped garlic. Place the tray in the oven and cook for 10 minutes.

To cook the fish, take the tray from the oven and give the tomatoes and mushrooms a squeeze to check that they are nearly cooked. Season the haddock with salt and pepper and drizzle generously with olive oil. Place the haddock skin side up on top of the mushrooms and tomatoes. Spread some of the béarnaise butter on top of the haddock.

Cover the fish with two more sheets of foil and fold the top and bottom foil edges together to make a sealed parcel. Place the tray back in the oven and cook for 12 minutes. Remove the tray from the oven and rest for 2 minutes.

To serve, carefully cut open the foil at the top (don't let the steam scald you). Using a fish slice, carefully lift the fish onto 4 warmed plates. Share the tomatoes and mushrooms equally between the plates and spoon the buttery sauce over the fish. Serve immediately.

Turbot is such a great fish to bake. Here I'm coating it with a seaweed and breadcrumb crust, which adds flavour and protects the fish from the direct heat of the oven. It's also perfect for soaking up the turbot's natural cooking juices. Using olive oil instead of butter in the classic hollandaise works really well – do give it a try. I like to serve this dish simply with boiled new potatoes and broccoli.

Turbot fillets, seaweed crust, olive oil and lime hollandaise

Serves 4

4 filleted turbot portions, about 180g each, skinned
100g plain flour, to dust
2 medium eggs, beaten
Sea salt and freshly ground black pepper

For the seaweed crust
100g fresh breadcrumbs
2 tbsp dried seaweed flakes
2 tbsp chopped flat-leaf parsley
Finely grated zest of 1 lime

For the lime hollandaise
175ml olive oil
Finely grated zest and juice of 1 lime
2 egg yolks
2 tbsp water

Preheat your oven to 220°C/Fan 205°C/Gas 7.

For the seaweed crust, put the breadcrumbs, seaweed, parsley and lime zest into a food processor with a pinch of salt and a generous grinding of black pepper. Blitz until the breadcrumbs start to go green, but don't overwork. Tip the breadcrumb mixture out onto a tray.

Check your fish fillets for any bone or sinew. Have the flour ready on a plate and the beaten eggs in a shallow bowl. One by one, dip one side of each fillet into the flour, then dip the same side into the egg. Finally lay the turbot fillets, coated side down, in the seaweed crumb mix and pat down gently. Leave the fillets like this until you are ready to cook them.

To make the lime hollandaise, warm the olive oil in a pan until tepid, then add half the lime zest and remove from the heat. Place the egg yolks in a medium heatproof bowl and add the lime juice and water. Stand the bowl over a pan of gently simmering water and whisk until the mixture thickens enough to form a ribbon when the beaters are lifted.

Remove the bowl from the pan and slowly whisk in the olive oil, in a thin, steady stream. Once all the oil is incorporated, season the hollandaise with salt and pepper to taste. Cover with a lid or a plate to prevent a skin forming and keep warm while you cook the fish.

To cook the fish, place the turbot fillets, crust uppermost, on an oiled baking tray and bake for 8–10 minutes until the fish is just cooked.

Carefully lift each turbot fillet onto a warmed plate. Sprinkle with the remaining lime zest and serve straight away, with the lime hollandaise.

These flatbreads go down well whenever I cook them for friends – I think it's because everyone loves a pizza and they come pretty close. Sardines work well, because of the lovely oiliness you get from them, but herrings or mackerel would be good too. You can vary the topping ingredients but make sure the mixture isn't too wet or the bread will be soggy. For a party, you could make a large flatbread – it will look amazing.

Sardine, pepper and shallot flatbreads

Makes 4

8 sardines, scaled, gutted
 and filleted
A little light olive oil, for oiling
 and drizzling
Sea salt and freshly ground
 black pepper

For the flatbread dough
250g self-raising flour, plus
 extra to dust
2 tsp sea salt
250g full-fat Greek yoghurt
1 tbsp chopped tender
 rosemary leaves
2 tbsp mature Cheddar, grated
1 garlic clove, peeled and
 chopped

For the topping
50ml olive oil
50g unsalted butter
4 banana shallots, peeled and
 sliced
2 red peppers, peeled,
 deseeded and sliced
2 garlic cloves, peeled and
 sliced
1 tender rosemary sprig,
 leaves picked and chopped
75ml red wine vinegar
50g caster sugar
1 tbsp small capers in brine,
 drained and rinsed
A bunch of basil, leaves
 picked and shredded

To make the flatbread dough, place all the ingredients in a bowl and mix well until evenly combined and the mixture forms a dough. Turn out onto a lightly floured surface and knead for 2 minutes. Cover with a clean damp cloth and set aside while you make the topping.

For the topping, heat a medium pan over a medium heat and add the olive oil and butter. When hot, add the shallots, peppers, garlic and rosemary. Cook, stirring, frequently, for 5 minutes, until the veg start to soften. Lower the heat and cook gently for a further 5 minutes.

Now add the wine vinegar and sugar and cook until the vinegar has reduced right down, then add the capers and season with salt and pepper to taste. Tip the mixture onto a tray and set aside to cool.

Preheat your oven to 220°C/Fan 205°C/Gas 7 and oil two large baking sheets with olive oil.

Divide the bread dough into 4 equal portions and shape each into a ball. Roll out each one to a round or oval, the thickness of a £1 coin. Lift onto the oiled trays.

Stir the shredded basil through the cooled shallot mixture, then divide it between the dough bases, making sure you spread it right to the edges. Bake for 10 minutes.

While the flatbreads are in the oven, oil and season your sardine fillets. Take the flatbreads from the oven and lay 4 sardine fillets on top of each one. Return to the oven and bake for another 8 minutes.

As you take the flatbreads from the oven, drizzle with a little olive oil. Serve at once.

Everyone has their own recipe for a fabulous fish pie. For me, it has to be one-third cod, one-third salmon and one-third smoked haddock. Too much cod and it's bland, too much smoked haddock and it dominates, too much salmon and it's greasy. As for those who make it posh with lobster, prawns and scallops, that's just a waste. I've cooked this recipe for two and I've cooked it for 200... I think it's bloody lovely! If you want some veg with it, you can't go wrong with buttered, minted peas and carrots.

My fish pie

Serves 8

For the mash
1.5kg floury potatoes, such
  as Maris Piper
100g butter
200ml milk

For the filling
300g cod fillet, skinned
300g smoked haddock fillet,
  skinned
300g salmon fillet, skinned
1 litre whole milk
100g butter
100g plain flour
2 tbsp finely diced shallots
2 tbsp gherkins, chopped
1 tbsp small capers in brine,
  drained and rinsed
2 tbsp chopped parsley
1 tbsp chopped tarragon
1 tbsp chopped chives
1 tbsp chopped chervil
Sea salt and freshly ground
  black pepper

For the topping
150g mature Cheddar, grated
8 medium eggs

For the mash, peel the potatoes and cut into even-sized chunks. Place in a large pan, cover with cold water, add a large pinch of salt and bring to the boil. Lower the heat and simmer for about 20 minutes, until tender.

Drain the potatoes and let them sit in the colander for a few minutes, then return to the pan. Mash until smooth and beat in the butter and milk. Season well with salt and pepper and set aside.

Preheat your oven to 180°C/Fan 165°C/Gas 4. For the filling, pour the milk into a large pan and bring to a simmer. Meanwhile, cut all the fish into chunks.

Melt the butter in a medium pan over a fairly low heat and stir in the flour. Cook, stirring, for a couple of minutes, being careful not to let it brown. Gradually stir in the hot milk. Bring to the boil, lower the heat and simmer for about 20 minutes. Take off the heat and stir in the shallots, gherkins, capers and herbs. Season the sauce with salt and pepper to taste. Add the fish and toss to combine.

Tip the seafood and sauce into a 30cm square (or similar) baking dish. Spoon or pipe the mashed potato on top and scatter over the cheese. Bake for 20 minutes until the topping is golden.

Meanwhile, bring another pan of water to the boil, then carefully lower in the eggs. Cook for 6 minutes, then drain and place under cold running water until the eggs are cool enough to handle. Peel the boiled eggs and cut in half.

When the pie is ready, remove from the oven and poke the halved boiled eggs into the potato topping. Serve straight away.

Bake

Great quality smoked haddock marries surprisingly well with curried lentils, and lime yoghurt lends a cooling, refreshing contrast. If you're not keen on smoked fish, use plain haddock, hake or cod – something with a good flake to it. And if you're not a fan of lentils, new potatoes work well.

Smoked haddock and curried lentils, lime yoghurt

Serves 4–6

2 sides of smoked haddock,
   500–600g each, skinned
   and pin-boned
100g unsalted butter, diced
50ml light rapeseed oil
Sea salt

For the curry paste

2 tsp coriander seeds
2 tsp cumin seeds
1 tsp fenugreek seeds
1 tsp yellow mustard seeds
4 garlic cloves, peeled
3 green chillies, halved and
   deseeded

For the lentils

400g Puy lentils
Light rapeseed oil for cooking
2 red onions, peeled and root
   removed, thinly sliced
50g fresh ginger, peeled and
   grated
2 garlic cloves, peeled and
   chopped
350g baby plum tomatoes,
   halved
100ml tamarind liquid (see
   note)
100ml coconut milk
50g soft brown sugar
A handful of coriander, leaves
   picked and roughly chopped
A handful of mint, leaves
   picked and roughly chopped

For the lime yoghurt

200g full-fat Greek yoghurt
Finely grated zest and juice
   of 1 lime

Preheat your oven to 200°C/Fan 185°C/Gas 6.

Oil a sheet of foil large enough to hold the smoked haddock in one layer. Dot the butter over the fish and then cover with another sheet of foil. Fold the edges together to form a sealed parcel and place on a baking tray. Bake for 15 minutes, then remove from the oven and set the sealed parcel to one side for 10 minutes to rest.

Meanwhile, for the curry paste, finely grind all the spices together in a spice grinder or with a pestle and mortar. Transfer to a small food processor, add the garlic and chillies and whiz to a fine paste, adding a few drops of water if needed. Season with a good pinch of salt.

To cook the lentils, put them into a pan, add water to cover and some salt. Bring to a simmer over a medium heat and allow to simmer for 10–15 minutes until just cooked. Drain and tip onto a tray to cool.

Heat a sauté pan and add a drizzle of oil. Add the onions, ginger and garlic and sweat for 2 minutes until starting to soften and colour. Add the curry paste and cook, stirring, for 2 minutes. Add the tomatoes and cook for 3 minutes until they start to break down. Add the tamarind liquid, coconut milk and sugar. Bring to a simmer and cook for 10 minutes.

For the yoghurt, in a bowl mix the yoghurt with the lime zest and juice and season with salt to taste.

Unwrap the parcel and flake the fish into a bowl, keeping it in chunky flakes. Reserve the cooking juices.

When ready to serve, add the lentils to the sauce and warm through for 2 minutes. Add half the herbs, the smoked haddock and reserved cooking juices and stir through carefully, trying not to break up the haddock flakes. Divide the curry between warmed bowls. Top with a generous spoonful of the lime yoghurt and scatter over the remaining herbs.

Note To make tamarind liquid, soak a piece (about 25g) of compressed block tamarind in 150ml warm water for 10 minutes, then strain through a fine sieve; discard the pulp.

Pasta bakes can be boring, but not this one! It's a fantastic way of using crab, especially as you include the tasty brown meat. Rice-shaped orzo pasta is particularly good here but other pasta works too (see note). I use the best Cornish crab I can get my mitts on but crab from anywhere is fine, so long as it's fresh. A shaved fennel and rocket salad tossed with a lemony dressing is a great accompaniment, as it cuts the richness perfectly.

Crab and saffron pasta bake

Serves 4

150g brown crabmeat
200g white crabmeat, picked
300g orzo pasta
200ml fish stock (see
  page 218)
150ml milk
300ml double cream
1 tsp saffron strands
35g brown breadcrumbs
30g mature Cheddar, grated

Preheat your oven to 180°C/Fan 165°C/Gas 4.

Bring a pan of salted water to the boil and add the pasta. Bring back to the boil and cook for 6–7 minutes, then drain. Rinse out the pan, then return the pasta to it. Add the fish stock, milk, cream and saffron. Bring to the boil, stirring all the time.

Add the brown crabmeat to the mixture and immediately turn off the heat. Stir well, then add the white crabmeat. Stir again, then tip the mixture into an oven dish.

Mix the breadcrumbs and grated cheese together and sprinkle over the pasta. Bake for 20–25 minutes until golden and bubbling.

Note You can use any shaped pasta, but you'll need to adjust the initial cooking time accordingly – the aim is to undercook the pasta by a couple of minutes at this stage.

This is real comfort food for me. It's the sort of dish I want on a chilly spring evening, with plenty of good crusty bread to mop up the juices. It doesn't need anything else. You might like to add some extra smoked fish, such as mackerel or haddock, with the salmon. You could also bake small portions in little individual baking dishes to serve as a starter.

Smoked salmon, cauliflower and asparagus bake

Serves 4

200g smoked salmon
50g unsalted butter
50g plain flour
200ml fish stock (see page 218)
200ml whole milk
12 asparagus spears, woody parts removed, cut in half
1 large cauliflower, broken into small florets
2 tsp English mustard
2 tbsp chopped parsley
1 tbsp chopped tarragon
100g mature Cheddar, grated
Sea salt and freshly ground black pepper

Preheat your oven to 200°C/Fan 185°C/Gas 6. Cut the smoked salmon into strips and set aside.

To make the sauce, melt the butter in a saucepan, add the flour and cook, stirring, for 3 minutes to make a roux. Heat the fish stock and milk together and add to the pan gradually, little by little, stirring all the time to avoid lumps. Once all the liquid is incorporated, cook the sauce over a low heat for 20 minutes, stirring every couple of minutes.

Meanwhile, bring a pan of salted water to the boil. Add the asparagus and blanch for 2 minutes. Remove with a slotted spoon and immediately plunge into a bowl of iced water to cool quickly. Blanch the cauliflower for 4 minutes and refresh in the same way.

When the vegetables are cold, drain well and arrange in an oven dish. Lay the smoked salmon over and in between the vegetables.

When the sauce is ready, stir in the mustard and chopped herbs. Season with salt and pepper to taste. Pour the sauce over the vegetables and scatter the grated cheese on top. Bake for 15 minutes until golden and bubbling. Serve on warmed plates, with bread and butter on the side.

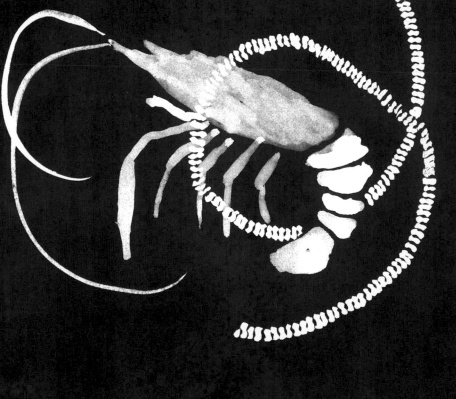

GRILL & BARBECUE

Grilling scampi (aka langoustines) topped with a savoury butter is one of the best ways to cook them in my view. All piled up on a plate, they look so inviting. The butter also works well with lobster, scallops or whole grilled plaice or lemon sole.

Scampi with saffron and olive butter

Serves 4

20 whole raw scampi, shell
  on, live or frozen

**For the saffron and olive
  butter**

½ tsp saffron strands
Finely grated zest and juice
  of I lemon
250g unsalted butter, softened
I shallot, peeled and chopped
I garlic clove, peeled and
  chopped
2 tbsp pitted black olives,
  chopped
20 basil leaves, finely sliced
Sea salt

To serve

2 lemons, halved

Place the scampi on a board. Split them in half lengthways from head to tail and remove the stomach and dark intestinal tract. Crack the claws and set aside.

To make the flavoured butter, put the saffron and lemon juice into a small pan and heat gently to infuse and encourage the saffron colour to bleed out.

Put the butter, shallot, garlic, olives, basil and lemon zest into a bowl and mix thoroughly until evenly blended. Spoon the butter onto a doubled sheet of greaseproof paper then wrap the greaseproof paper around it, shaping it into a cylinder about 3cm in diameter as you go. Twist the ends to secure and chill until ready to use. (The butter can be prepared ahead and frozen at this stage.)

Preheat your grill to high. Meanwhile, cut the butter into thin discs (you'll need 40 in total). Place the 4 lemon halves, cut side up, on a grill tray and grill until they start to colour.

Add the scampi to the grill tray, flesh side uppermost, with the claws. Place a disc of butter on each scampi half and grill for 4–5 minutes until the scampi are cooked and the lemon halves are tinged with brown, basting the scampi with the melting butter occasionally.

Divide the scampi between warmed bowls. Add the lemon halves and serve straight away.

Grill and barbecue

Grill and barbecue

Angels on horseback are typically served as a classic hors d'oeuvre or canapé. In the summer, I like to cook them on the barbecue and serve them with a glass of bubbles or, I think, even better, a beer. I use our farmed Rock oysters for this dish; I wouldn't use a native oyster for cooking. The pea pâté is really refreshing with the salty oyster and bacon, and it also makes a great vegetarian course on its own with some sourdough.

Angels on horseback, pea pâté

Serves 4
20 rock oysters, shucked
20 rashers of smoked streaky
  bacon
A drizzle of olive oil

For the pea pâté
300g freshly podded or frozen
  peas
100g full-fat cream cheese
100g full-fat Greek yoghurt
Juice of 1 lime
20 mint leaves, shredded
Sea salt and freshly ground
  black pepper

To finish
Extra virgin olive oil

To make the pea pâté, bring a pan of salted water to the boil and have a bowl of iced water ready. Once the water is boiling, add the peas and cook for 2 minutes. Drain and then plunge the peas into the ice-cold water to cool quickly so they keep their colour. When cold, drain well.

Tip the peas into a food processor and add the cream cheese, yoghurt, lime juice and mint. Blend for 3 minutes until smooth, then season with salt and pepper to taste. Spoon the pâté into a serving bowl, cover and place in the fridge to set.

Light the barbecue about 30 minutes before you want to cook the oysters, or preheat the grill. Meanwhile, check the oysters for any fragments of shell. Lay a rasher of bacon on a board, place an oyster at one end and roll up to enclose the oyster. Thread onto a skewer to hold it together. Repeat with the rest of the oysters, threading 5 wrapped oysters onto each of 4 skewers.

To cook, drizzle the oysters with a little olive oil and then carefully place them on the barbecue grid or grill tray. Cook for 2 minutes on each side.

Once cooked, place the skewered oysters on a platter. Add a drizzle of olive oil to the pea pâté and serve with the skewers.

This is a fun dish to serve as a warm canapé or starter. I really like the way oysters – and their shells – give off an amazing aroma of the sea when you grill them. I've also cooked these oysters on a barbecue – the additional smoke works wonders, so give it a go if you get the chance. Scallops in the shell and half lobsters are also great served this way.

Oysters with smoked hollandaise sauce

Serves 4 as a starter

12 live rock oysters
About 400g rock salt for
  grilling, plus extra to serve
1 lemon, peeled, pith removed
  and cut into segments

**For the smoked hollandaise
  sauce**

250g smoked butter
3 egg yolks
Juice of ½ lemon
Cayenne pepper, to taste
Sea salt
Dill leaves, finely chopped,
  to finish

Open the oysters and prise off the top shell. Drain off the juices. Cut the muscle to release the oyster but leave it in the rounded shell; check for any fragments of shell.

Preheat your grill to its highest setting and line a grill tray with enough salt to sit the oysters on to hold them steady. (If you don't have enough salt, make small foil rings to support the oyster shells.)

To make the hollandaise, melt the smoked butter in a pan over a medium heat until it begins to bubble, then remove from the heat and leave to cool until tepid. Meanwhile, put the egg yolks and lemon juice in a heatproof bowl over a pan of hot water set over a medium-low heat, making sure the base of the bowl is not touching the water. Whisk until the mixture thickens enough to form ribbons when you lift the beaters.

Remove the bowl from the pan and slowly whisk in the melted butter. Once it is all incorporated, season the hollandaise with cayenne pepper and salt. Taste and adjust the seasoning as necessary, adding a little more lemon juice too, if you think it is needed. Keep warm while you grill the oysters.

Lay the oysters in their shells on the prepared tray and place under the grill for 3 minutes. Remove from the grill. Place a lemon segment on each oyster and then spoon on some hollandaise. Put back under the grill for a minute or so, until the hollandaise is just starting to brown.

Finish with a sprinkling of chopped dill and a little more cayenne pepper. Serve immediately, on a bed of salt.

Grill and barbecue

Recently, as I was eating lobster, its amazing smell mingled with the aroma of spices cooking in the kitchen and took me back to a once-in-a-lifetime family holiday in Jamaica, when I was twelve. I wanted to create something like the Jamaican dishes I enjoyed all those years ago. The lobsters we get here are very different from those in the Caribbean. I've toned down the heat and spice to allow the special flavours of our lobsters to come through, but if spice is your thing, feel free to add more!

Barbecued jerk lobster with coconut rice

Serves 2

2 live lobsters, 600–800g each

For the jerk sauce
A drizzle of sunflower oil
2 garlic cloves, peeled and chopped
2 tsp chopped fresh ginger
1 bunch of spring onions, trimmed and finely sliced
1 red chilli, deseeded and chopped
½ tsp ground cinnamon
½ tsp freshly grated nutmeg
½ tsp ground allspice
1 tsp chopped rosemary
1 bay leaf
Finely grated zest and juice of 1 lime
Finely grated zest and juice of 1 orange
50g caster sugar
2 tbsp dark soy sauce
200ml chicken stock (see page 218)
1 tbsp chopped coriander leaves
Sea salt

For the coconut rice
140g basmati rice
A drizzle of sunflower oil
4 spring onions, trimmed and finely sliced
1 garlic clove, peeled and finely sliced
100ml coconut milk
100ml chicken stock (or water)

To serve
2 limes, halved
Chopped coriander

Put the lobsters in the freezer for an hour before cooking to sedate them. Wash the rice in several changes of water, then leave to soak in cold water for 30 minutes.

To make the sauce, heat a large pan over a medium heat, then add the oil. When hot, add the garlic, ginger, spring onions and chilli and fry for 2 minutes. Add the spices, rosemary, bay leaf and citrus zests and cook for 2 minutes, then add the sugar, soy sauce, citrus juices and stock. Bring to a simmer and let bubble for about 5 minutes to reduce and thicken. Add a pinch of salt and the chopped coriander. Set aside to cool.

To kill the lobsters, firmly insert the tip of a strong cook's knife into the cross on the head. Now carefully cut the lobsters in half lengthways, from head to tail. Remove the stomach sac from the head and the dark intestinal thread running along the length of the tail. Crack the claws. Lay the lobster halves on a tray and spoon half the jerk sauce over them. Leave to marinate for 30 minutes, while you light and heat up the barbecue.

Meanwhile, drain the rice. Heat a pan (with a tight-fitting lid) and add the oil. When it is hot, add the spring onions and garlic and sweat for 2 minutes. Add the rice and cook, stirring, for 1 minute. Pour in the coconut milk and stock and bring to a simmer. Turn the heat down low, put the lid on and cook for 10 minutes. Take the pan off the heat and leave to stand, covered, for 5 minutes.

To cook the lobsters, when the barbecue coals are white hot, place the lobster claws on the barbecue grid and cook for 3–4 minutes. Turn the lobsters claws over and add the lobster tails, shell side down, and the lime halves, cut side down. Cook for 3–4 minutes, then turn the lobster tails over and cook for a further 2 minutes.

When the lobster is cooked, transfer to a warmed platter and spoon on some more jerk sauce. Sprinkle with chopped coriander and add the lime halves. Fluff up the rice with a fork and serve on the side.

This octopus dish really hits the spot. I've taken one of my favourite Spanish dishes, *ajo blanco* (white gazpacho) and used it as a bread sauce for the charred octopus. The flavours are great together so give it a go. If you can't get hold of octopus, large squid can be cooked in the same way, or, even quicker, small raw squid or scallops can be added straight to the barbecue or grill.

Seared octopus, almond and sherry vinegar bread sauce

Serves 4

1 octopus (double sucker species), about 1kg (defrosted if frozen)
Olive oil for cooking
4 shallots, peeled and chopped
5 garlic cloves, peeled and crushed
2 rosemary sprigs
100ml fino or other dry sherry
Finely grated zest of 1 lemon
Sea salt and freshly ground black pepper

For the almond and sherry vinegar bread sauce

100g whole almonds, blanched and skinned
120g good crustless white or wholemeal bread, in chunks
2 garlic cloves, peeled and finely chopped
6 tbsp sherry vinegar
300ml extra virgin olive oil

To garnish

A bunch of watercress, leaves picked
A small bunch of seedless green grapes, sliced
2 tbsp chopped parsley
1 tbsp chopped chives
Olive oil to drizzle

First you need to braise the octopus to tenderise it. Heat a pan large enough to hold the octopus (with a tight-fitting lid) and add a drizzle of olive oil. When hot, add the shallots, garlic and rosemary. Cook for 2 minutes, then add the sherry, followed by the octopus and lemon zest. Put the lid on and cook gently for 1 hour, or until the octopus is tender.

In the meantime, make the bread sauce. Preheat your oven to 190°C/ Fan 175°C/Gas 5. Scatter the almonds on a baking tray and roast in the oven for 5 minutes. Put the bread into a bowl, add water to cover and leave to soak for 5–10 minutes. Put the roasted almonds and garlic into a food processor and pulse until smooth. Squeeze the bread to remove all excess water, then add to the food processor with a good pinch of salt. With the motor running, add the sherry vinegar, followed by the olive oil in a steady stream. Once the oil is all incorporated, taste and add more salt and vinegar if you like. Refrigerate until needed.

When the octopus is cooked, lift it out on a tray and leave until cool enough to handle. Cut off and reserve the tentacles, discarding the beak. Slit open the main body and remove the ink sac, stomach and eyes carefully. Cut the body meat into 4 equal pieces. Skewer these and the tentacles in portions. Oil the octopus and season with salt and pepper, then set aside until ready to cook.

Light the barbecue about 30 minutes before you want to cook, or preheat the grill. When the coals are white hot or the grill is ready, carefully place the octopus skewers on the barbecue grid or grill pan and cook for 2–3 minutes on each side until nicely coloured and charred.

To serve, share the watercress and octopus between 4 plates. Toss the sliced grapes and chopped herbs together with a drizzle of olive oil and a little salt, then spoon over and around the octopus. Put a spoonful of bread sauce on each plate. Serve hot or cold.

The flavour that smoking coals give scampi is quite something and cannot be recreated with any other cooking method. You just need to be careful as you turn or handle the scampi, as they are quite fragile. The tomato and chilli chutney is a great accompaniment; if you have any left, it will keep in the fridge for a few weeks. Large raw prawns and lobster are also excellent cooked this way.

Barbecued scampi with tomato and chilli chutney

Serves 4

16 medium or large raw
  scampi, shell on, live or
  frozen

For the seasoning
1 tsp coriander seeds
2 tsp salt
Finely grated zest of 2 lemons
1 tsp dried oregano

For the tomato chutney
Olive oil for cooking
2 red onions, peeled and
  finely chopped
2 tsp coriander seeds
4 garlic cloves, peeled and
  finely chopped
8 red chillies, deseeded and
  finely chopped
100g fresh ginger, peeled and
  finely grated
700g ripe plum tomatoes,
  blanched, skinned and
  chopped
200g dark brown sugar
100ml red wine vinegar
50ml balsamic vinegar
2 tsp salt

To make the chutney, heat a large saucepan over a medium heat and add a drizzle of olive oil. When hot, add the onions with the coriander seeds and cook for 6–8 minutes until the onions are softened and just starting to brown. Add the garlic, chillies and ginger and cook for 4 minutes. Now add the tomatoes, sugar, both vinegars and the salt. Cook, stirring occasionally, for 20 minutes until the mixture is well reduced and sticky; it will start to catch on the bottom of the pan. Remove from the heat.

Using a stick blender, blitz the chutney briefly to break it up a bit, but don't go too far – it should have some texture. Taste for seasoning and add more salt if you think it needs it. Transfer the chutney to a bowl and allow to cool, then refrigerate.

To prepare the seasoning for the scampi, toast the coriander seeds in a dry pan over a medium heat for a minute or two until fragrant, then remove from the heat and add the salt, lemon zest and oregano. Using a pestle and mortar or spice grinder, grind the mixture until fine. Set aside.

Light your barbecue 30 minutes before you are planning to cook. Place the scampi on a board. Split them in half lengthways from head to tail and remove the stomach and dark intestinal tract. Crack the claws and set aside.

Once the coals are white hot, sprinkle the scampi all over with the prepared seasoning and place them on the barbecue grid, cut side down. Cook for 2 minutes, then carefully turn them over and cook for another 2 minutes.

To serve, place the scampi on a large platter with a pot of the chutney and let everyone help themselves.

I think lemon sole are one of the most underrated fish. When they are at their best, between February and May, they are magnificent grilled whole. A zesty herb butter flavoured with capers and anchovies is the perfect complement. All you need is some minted new potatoes on the side.

Lemon sole, green sauce butter

Serves 4

4 lemon sole, 500–700g each
Olive oil for cooking
Sea salt and freshly ground
  black pepper

For the green sauce butter

1 shallot, peeled and finely
  chopped
1 garlic clove, peeled, halved
  (germ removed) and
  chopped
2 tbsp chopped flat-leaf
  parsley
2 tbsp chopped rocket leaves
1 tbsp chopped mint
1 tbsp chopped basil
2 anchovy fillets in oil,
  drained and chopped
1 tsp small capers in brine,
  drained, rinsed and chopped
½ tsp English mustard
Finely grated zest and juice
  of ½ lemon
300g unsalted butter, softened

For the garnish

300ml sunflower oil for deep-
  frying
2 tbsp large capers, drained,
  rinsed and chopped

For the green sauce butter, put all the chopped ingredients into a bowl with the English mustard, lemon zest and juice. Add the softened butter and mix thoroughly until evenly blended. Season with salt and pepper to taste. Spoon the butter onto a doubled sheet of greaseproof paper then wrap the greaseproof paper around it, shaping it into a cylinder about 3cm in diameter as you go. Twist the ends to secure and chill until ready to use. (The butter can be prepared ahead and frozen at this stage.)

For the garnish, heat the sunflower oil in a small, deep, heavy pan over a medium heat to 180°C. Add the capers and fry for 1 minute until crispy. Remove with a slotted spoon and drain on kitchen paper; keep warm.

Preheat your grill to high. Oil a grill tray large enough to comfortably hold the fish (or cook them two at a time). Oil the fish, season all over with salt and pepper and place on the grill tray, dark side up. Cut the butter into discs and lay on top of the fish.

Cook the sole under the grill for 10–12 minutes. To check for doneness, insert a small knife into the thickest part of the fish, near the head, and pull at the bone. You should see the fillet coming away from the bone; if not, cook it for another couple of minutes or so until it does.

To serve, carefully lift the fish onto warmed plates and spoon over the butter, along with any cooking juices left on the grill tray. Finish with the deep-fried capers and serve at once.

The sense of smell is amazing. When I cook this, the aroma takes me right back to 1999 when I was preparing a similar dish at Rick Stein's The Seafood Restaurant in Padstow. The smell of red mullet cooking is unlike any other fish – it is utterly unique. That, and the smell of the girolles pan-frying with garlic and parsley, is enough to bring any food lover to their knees.

Red mullet with girolles and roasted garlic aïoli

Serves 4

4 red mullet, 500–600g each, scaled, filleted and pin-boned
Olive oil for grilling
Sea salt and freshly ground black pepper

For the roasted garlic aïoli
1 garlic bulb
2 egg yolks
Finely grated zest and juice of 1 lemon
400ml olive oil

For the girolles
400g girolles, cleaned and halved or quartered if large
A drizzle of olive oil
100g unsalted butter
2 shallots, peeled and chopped
1 garlic clove, peeled and finely chopped
75ml sherry vinegar
3 tbsp chopped flat-leaf parsley

Preheat your oven to 200°C/Fan 185°C/Gas 6. For the roasted garlic, wrap the garlic bulb in some foil, place it in an oven dish and bake for 45 minutes until soft. Unwrap the garlic and leave until cool enough to handle. Separate the cloves and squeeze out the soft garlic pulp.

To make the aïoli, put the egg yolks, lemon zest and juice, and the roasted garlic pulp into a small food processor. Blend briefly to combine then, with the motor running, slowly add the olive oil in a thin, steady stream through the funnel until it is all incorporated and the sauce is emulsified. Season with salt and pepper, blend for a further 30 seconds, then taste and adjust the seasoning if necessary. Transfer to a bowl, cover and refrigerate until ready to serve.

Preheat your grill to its highest setting.

To cook the girolles, heat a large frying pan over a medium heat, then add the olive oil and butter. When bubbling, add the girolles and fry for 2 minutes.

At the same time, brush the red mullet fillets with oil, season them and place skin side up under the grill.

Now add the shallots and garlic to the girolles, cook for another minute, then add the sherry vinegar. Toss in the parsley, season with salt and pepper and remove from the heat.

By now, your red mullet fillets will be colouring and almost ready – they will take about 4 minutes. To check, lift one up carefully and turn it over. The flesh should be white with no sign of rawness.

Place a large spoonful of the roasted garlic aïoli in the middle of each warmed plate and add a red mullet fillet. Share the girolles between the plates and serve straight away.

Grill and barbecue

This is a really nice dish for late summer when bass is great, courgettes are aplenty and herbs are thriving. The lovely saltiness of the air-dried ham (Parma or Bayonne), with the zingy lemon and fresh herbs, works brilliantly with the bass. If the weather's good, you could barbecue the bass whole and just serve it with the courgette salad and dressing.

Bass with air-dried ham, courgettes, lemon and herbs

Serves 4

1 bass, 1.5–2kg, gutted, scaled, filleted and pin-boned
2 tbsp olive oil, plus extra to drizzle and dress the courgettes
1 white onion, peeled and diced
3 garlic cloves, peeled, halved (germ removed) and sliced
8 slices of air-dried ham, cut into strips
300ml fish stock (see page 218)
250ml double cream
3 courgettes
1 tbsp chopped tarragon
1 tbsp chopped flat-leaf parsley
1 tbsp chopped dill
1 tbsp chopped chives
Finely grated zest and juice of 1 lemon
2 tbsp Dijon mustard
Sea salt and freshly ground black pepper

To make the sauce, heat a medium pan over a medium heat and add the 2 tbsp olive oil. When it is hot, add the onion and garlic and cook for 3 minutes to soften. Add the ham and cook for a further 4 minutes until it is starting to crisp.

Pour in the fish stock, bring to a simmer and let bubble until reduced by half. Add the cream, bring back to a simmer and cook for 10 minutes until the sauce starts to thicken.

Meanwhile finely slice the courgettes lengthways, on a mandoline if you have one (or veg peeler if not), and place in a bowl. Add the herbs, with half of the lemon zest and juice. Drizzle with olive oil, season with salt and pepper and toss well.

Preheat your grill to high.

To finish the sauce, add the remaining lemon juice and mustard and season with a little salt and pepper. Bring to a simmer, then taste and adjust the seasoning. Set aside while you cook the fish.

Cut the bass fillets in half to give 4 equal portions and place skin side up on a grill tray. Drizzle with olive oil, sprinkle on the remaining lemon zest and season with salt and pepper. Grill the fish for 5–7 minutes.

Meanwhile, give the courgettes another toss and then drain in a colander set over a bowl to collect the dressing. Remove the fish from the grill and leave to rest and finish cooking on the tray for 1 minute.

Spoon the sauce onto 4 warmed plates. Pile two-thirds of the courgettes in the centre and lay a portion of bass on top. Arrange the remaining courgette ribbons on the fish and finish with a spoonful or two of the dressing. Serve at once.

If it's warm enough for a barbecue I always look out for fresh sardines, as they are amazing cooked over coals. The pepper salad goes perfectly and I love the fact that you can use the barbecue for that too. If you fancy it, you can add a few other veggies to the peppers as well, such as courgettes or mushrooms – I usually grab whatever is to hand. If you can't get sardines, mackerel is a great alternative. And if the weather's iffy, use the grill instead.

Smoked paprika sardines, marinated pepper salad

Serves 4

12 fresh sardines, scaled and
  gutted
4 tsp sweet smoked paprika
2 tsp salt
About 100ml olive oil

**For the marinated
  pepper salad**
2 red peppers
1 yellow pepper
1 green pepper
2 red onions, peeled and each
  cut into 6 wedges
3 garlic cloves, peeled and
  finely chopped
2 thyme sprigs, leaves picked
  and chopped
20 basil leaves, finely sliced
100ml red wine vinegar
100ml extra virgin olive oil
A couple of handfuls of rocket
  leaves
Sea salt and freshly ground
  black pepper

To serve
2 lemons, halved

For the pepper salad, peel the skin from the peppers, using a vegetable peeler (don't worry if you don't get all the skin off). Halve, core and deseed the peppers, then cut into bite-sized pieces. Place in a bowl with the onion wedges, garlic, thyme, basil, wine vinegar and olive oil. Season with salt and pepper and leave to marinate for 15–20 minutes.

Light your barbecue about 30 minutes before you want to begin cooking (or preheat the grill). When it is almost ready, thread the peppers and onions onto skewers. Reserve the oil and vinegar remaining in the bowl for the dressing.

When the barbecue coals are white hot (or the grill is ready), lay the vegetable skewers on the grid (or grill tray) and cook for 6–8 minutes, turning occasionally, until the peppers are charred and soft. Slide the vegetables off the skewers into a bowl and set aside to cool.

Meanwhile, season the sardines with the smoked paprika and salt and drizzle all over with olive oil. Lay them on the barbecue grid or grill tray and cook for 3 minutes on each side, turning carefully.

To serve, dress the peppers and onions with the reserved oil and vinegar mixture. Add the rocket leaves and toss to combine. Serve the sardines with the pepper salad, lemon halves and a sprinkling of salt.

Grill and barbecue

Monkfish marinated and cooked this way is particularly special. This fish really benefits from being cooked on the bone, as it helps to stop the flesh shrinking too much. It works well on the barbecue, but make sure you get the coals white hot or it will stick and you'll lose some of the marinade as a result. The spiced butter dressing enhances the flavour perfectly.

Monkfish on the bone, spiced butter and fennel

Serves 4

1.2–1.5kg monkfish tail on
  the bone, trimmed of sinew
  and skin
100ml sunflower oil
Finely grated zest of 2 lemons
½ tsp cayenne pepper
½ tsp freshly grated nutmeg
1 tender rosemary sprig,
  leaves picked and finely
  chopped
Sea salt and freshly ground
  black pepper

**For the spiced butter
  dressing**

200g unsalted butter
1 rosemary sprig
Finely grated zest and juice
  of 2 lemons
½ tsp cayenne pepper
½ tsp freshly grated nutmeg
4 shallots, peeled and
  chopped
2 large gherkins, finely
  chopped
2 tsp small capers in brine,
  drained and rinsed
4 tbsp chopped flat-leaf
  parsley

For the fennel

2 fennel bulbs, tough outer
  layer removed, cut into
  quarters
Olive oil to drizzle

Place the monkfish in a dish or large plastic container with a lid. Add the oil, lemon zest, cayenne, nutmeg, rosemary, salt and pepper. Turn the fish to coat, cover with a plate or lid and leave to marinate in the fridge for at least 2 (or up to 6) hours.

If you are barbecuing, light your barbecue at least 30 minutes before you plan to cook, or preheat the grill.

For the spiced butter dressing, heat the butter and rosemary in a pan over a medium heat until the butter has melted and begins to turn brown. Immediately take the pan off the heat and add the lemon zest, cayenne, nutmeg, a pinch of salt and the shallots. Remove the rosemary.

For the fennel, bring a large pan of salted water to the boil. Add the fennel and cook for 6–8 minutes until it starts to soften but is still quite firm. Drain and place on a tray to cool. Drizzle with olive oil and season.

When the coals are white hot or the grill is ready, remove the monkfish from the marinade and lay on the barbecue grid or grill rack. Cook for 4 minutes, then turn the fish over and cook for a further 4 minutes. Remove and set aside to rest on a warmed plate while you barbecue or grill the fennel for 5 minutes, turning to colour as necessary.

Meanwhile, finish the dressing. Put the lemon juice, gherkins, capers and chopped parsley into a small pan and add any cooking juices from the grill tray. Now add the spiced butter and give the dressing a good stir. Taste and adjust the seasoning. Heat the dressing until it is just too hot to hold your finger in it, then remove from the heat.

To serve, briefly put the monkfish back on the barbecue or under the grill to warm through for a couple of minutes. Place the fennel and the monkfish on a warmed platter and spoon on the spiced butter dressing. Serve in the centre of the table and let everyone help themselves.

Grill and barbecue

Monkfish is the perfect fish to cook on a griddle or barbecue, because it can handle big flavours and has a firm texture that responds well to aggressive cooking. It's essential to make sure that whatever you are cooking the monkfish on is red hot; if not it will stick and you won't get a lovely charred finish to the outside. If you're using wooden skewers, pre-soak them in cold water for 30 minutes or so, to prevent them burning before the monkfish is cooked.

Monkfish satay

Serves 4

600g monkfish fillet, trimmed of sinew and skin, cut into chunks
2 tbsp coriander seeds
2 garlic cloves, peeled and finely chopped
2 tbsp finely grated fresh ginger
3 lemongrass stalks, coarse outer layers removed, finely chopped
2 tbsp sunflower oil
2 tsp soy sauce
2 tsp fish sauce
Grated zest of 1 lime (use the juice for the sauce)
Sea salt and freshly ground black pepper

For the peanut sauce
A drizzle of sunflower oil
6 shallots or 2 banana shallots, peeled and finely chopped
4 garlic cloves, peeled and finely chopped
2 red chillies, deseeded and finely chopped
2 tbsp brown sugar
1 tbsp fish sauce
200ml coconut milk
160g unsalted peanuts, roasted and finely chopped
Juice of 1 lime

To serve
1 lime, cut into quarters

For the marinade, toast the coriander seeds in a dry pan over a medium heat for a minute or two until fragrant. Using a pestle and mortar or spice grinder, grind the seeds to a powder. Add the garlic, ginger and lemongrass and grind again. Add the oil, soy sauce, fish sauce and lime zest and mix well.

Lay the monkfish chunks in a suitable plastic container and coat all over with the marinade. Cover with the lid and refrigerate for 1 hour. If you are barbecuing, light your barbecue 30 minutes before you intend to cook.

Meanwhile, make the peanut sauce. Heat a medium pan over a medium heat, then add the oil. When it is hot, add the shallots, garlic and chillies and sweat for 3 minutes. Stir in the sugar and cook for a further 3 minutes, then add the fish sauce and coconut milk. Bring to the boil and let bubble for a couple of minutes. Stir in the peanuts and lime juice, then season with salt and pepper to taste. Keep warm (or allow to cool if preparing ahead and reheat to serve).

When the monkfish is ready, thread 4–5 chunks onto each of 4 skewers. If using a char-griddle, heat up over a high heat. When the char-grill is smoking or the barbecue coals are white hot, carefully lay the monkfish on the griddle or grid and cook for 2 minutes on each side.

Serve the monkfish on or off the skewers with lime wedges and the peanut sauce in a bowl on the side. Accompany with plain rice and a leafy side salad.

Grill and barbecue

Monkfish is probably the best fish to barbecue, but it does benefit from a little help flavourwise. Here I'm using Indian spices to give it a kick and bring the fish alive. The spicy cauliflower pickle and refreshing ginger and coriander yoghurt are ideal accompaniments.

Monkfish, cauliflower pickle, ginger and coriander yoghurt

Serves 4

4 monkfish tails on the bone, 200–300g each, trimmed of sinew and skin
1 tbsp mild curry powder
1 tbsp cumin seeds
1 tbsp coriander seeds
½ tbsp sea salt

For the pickle
A drizzle of sunflower oil
1 small cauliflower, cut into florets
1 fennel bulb, tough outer layer removed, thinly sliced (ideally on a mandoline)
1 red onion, peeled and thinly sliced (ideally on a mandoline)
2 green chillies, halved, deseeded and thinly sliced
200ml white wine vinegar
1 tsp salt
1 tsp ground cumin
1 tsp ground coriander seeds
Rapeseed oil to dress
2 tbsp chopped coriander

For the ginger and coriander yoghurt
200g full-fat Greek yoghurt
3 tbsp ginger juice (see note)
2 tbsp chopped coriander
Salt

First, make the pickle. Heat a frying pan over a medium heat and add the oil. When hot, add the cauliflower florets and sweat for a few minutes without colouring until they start to soften slightly. Add the fennel, onion and chillies and heat for a minute, then tip into a bowl.

Put the wine vinegar, salt and spices into a pan and bring to the boil, then strain the hot liquid over the cauliflower mixture. Cover the bowl with a disc of greaseproof paper pushed down to keep the vegetables submerged and set aside to cool completely.

For the monkfish, toast the spices in a dry pan over a medium heat for a minute until fragrant. Using a pestle and mortar or spice grinder, grind the toasted spices. Once the spice mix has cooled down, stir in the salt.

Coat the monkfish all over with the spice mixture and leave to marinate in the fridge for at least 30 minutes and up to 3 hours.

For the yoghurt, mix the yoghurt, ginger juice and chopped coriander together in a bowl and season with salt to taste. Cover and refrigerate until ready to serve.

If you are barbecuing, light your barbecue 30 minutes before you plan to cook, or preheat the grill. When the coals are white hot or the grill is ready, lay the monkfish tails on the barbecue grid or grill rack and cook for 4–5 minutes on each side, turning carefully.

Meanwhile, to finish the pickle, drain the cauliflower mixture and return to the bowl. Dress with a generous glug of rapeseed oil and toss through the chopped coriander. Season with salt to taste and mix well.

Serve the fish with a generous spoonful of the cauliflower pickle and the ginger and coriander yoghurt on the side.

Note To make the ginger juice, grate 150g freshly peeled ginger and squeeze tightly in a piece of muslin over a bowl to extract the juice.

Hake deserves to be more popular. It's an excellent variety for coaxing non-fish eaters and children to eat fish, especially if you serve it this way. The lovely bacon, hazelnut and earthy leek flavours merge as the fish cooks and the juices that collect in the grill pan are amazing. You could make this dish with any member of the cod family.

Hake with bacon, hazelnuts and leeks

Serves 4

4 filleted portions of hake, about 180g each, skin on
8 medium leeks, dark green part removed, well washed
8 rashers of smoked streaky bacon
100g blanched hazelnuts
Olive oil for cooking
Sea salt and freshly ground black pepper

For the dressing

1 shallot, peeled and finely chopped
1 garlic clove, peeled, halved (germ removed) and finely chopped
1 tbsp English mustard
3 tbsp verjus or lemon juice
3 tbsp water
400ml light olive oil

To finish

2 tbsp chopped flat-leaf parsley

To cook the leeks, bring a large pan of salted water to the boil over a medium heat. Cut the leeks across in half, add to the pan and cook for 12 minutes until tender (I like my leeks well cooked, not al dente).

Preheat your grill to medium. Season the hake portions with salt and pepper; set aside.

Lay the bacon on a grill tray and cook for about 5 minutes until crispy, turning halfway. Save any bacon fat on the tray, to add to the dressing.

Drain the leeks thoroughly and transfer to a shallow grillproof dish (large enough to hold the leeks in a single layer). Leave to cool slightly.

To make the dressing, put the shallot, garlic, mustard, verjus or lemon juice and water into a blender. Blend briefly to combine then, with the motor running, slowly add the olive oil in a thin, steady stream through the funnel until it is all incorporated and the dressing is emulsified. Add the retained bacon fat too. Pour the dressing over the leeks.

Scatter the hazelnuts on a grill tray and toast them under the grill until golden all over, turning as necessary to colour evenly. Tip the nuts onto a board and chop them roughly. Do the same to the bacon. Sprinkle the bacon and nuts over the leeks.

Lay the hake portions on top of the leeks and place under the grill. Cook for 6–8 minutes, depending on the thickness of the fish.

Either serve on a large warmed platter in the middle of the table and let everyone help themselves, or place on individual plates. Finish with a scattering of chopped parsley. I like this best with mash, but it is also good with new potatoes.

I get asked quite often what my final meal would be, which is a bit concerning. I'd rather be asked what would be my favourite thing to eat. Barbecued mackerel straight out of the sea and cooked on the beach has to be the answer. There's nothing quite like it: the freshness of the fish, the oiliness of the flesh and the blistering of the skin from the hot coals. Oh, and the lovely smokiness. The barbecue sauce is something of a classic in my kitchens. If you have any left, it will keep in a bottle in the fridge for up to a week, or you can freeze it.

Mackerel with barbecue sauce

Serves 4

4 large or 8 small mackerel, gutted

For the rub

2 tsp dried chilli flakes
3 tsp fennel seeds
1 tsp black peppercorns
Grated zest of 2 oranges (use the juice for the sauce)
3 tsp sea salt
3 tsp chopped rosemary

For 'my' barbecue sauce

A drizzle of olive oil
2 shallots, peeled and chopped
8 garlic cloves, peeled and chopped
3 green chillies, deseeded and chopped
A bunch of tarragon, leaves picked and chopped
8 rosemary sprigs, leaves picked and chopped
A small bunch of parsley, leaves picked and chopped
3 tbsp fennel seeds
Grated zest and juice of 2 oranges
100g soft brown sugar
150ml red wine vinegar
200ml freshly squeezed orange juice
3 tsp English mustard
400g tin good quality plum tomatoes
Sea salt and freshly ground black pepper

To prepare the rub, toast the spices in a dry pan over a medium heat for a minute or so until fragrant and starting to crackle a bit. Add the orange zest, salt and rosemary and heat for 30 seconds. Tip the contents of the pan into a mortar and grind with the pestle until fine. Leave to cool.

Slash the skin of the mackerel 3 or 4 times on each side and place the fish on a tray. Sprinkle all over with the spice mixture and rub it into the slashes. Leave to marinate in the fridge for 1 hour.

To make the barbecue sauce, heat a sauté pan over a medium heat and add the olive oil. When hot, add the shallots, garlic and chillies and sweat for 3 minutes. Stir in the chopped herbs, fennel seeds and orange zest and cook for another minute. Add the sugar and wine vinegar and stir until the sugar is dissolved, then let bubble to reduce until syrupy.

Add the orange juice, mustard and tomatoes with their juice. Bring to a simmer and let bubble until the liquid has reduced by half. Taste, then season with salt and pepper as required.

Tip the contents of the pan into a food processor and blitz for 3 minutes. Strain the sauce through a sieve into a bowl and leave to cool.

Light your barbecue 30 minutes before you plan on eating. When the coals are white hot, place the mackerel on the barbecue grid. Cook for 3 minutes on one side, then carefully turn the fish over and cook on the other side for 3 minutes. (Alternatively, you can cook the mackerel under a hot grill.)

Carefully lift the fish onto a serving platter, using a big fish slice, not tongs – mackerel is too delicate for these. Serve immediately, with my barbecue sauce on the side.

On a visit to the Basque region of Spain, I sat outside a fantastic restaurant in Getaria, and watched huge turbots being cooked on a magnificent barbecue. The taste was something else and I was determined to try and recreate the dish when I got home. Cooking a whole turbot is something you should have a go at; I know it's not cheap but it will be worth every penny, I promise. The potatoes are a simple Basque staple.

Turbot 'Getaria', Basque potatoes

Serves 6

1 turbot, about 3kg
500ml olive oil
300ml white wine vinegar
Sea salt and freshly ground
  black pepper

For the Basque potatoes

3 large potatoes, peeled and
  sliced
Olive oil for cooking
1 white onion, peeled and
  chopped
2 garlic cloves, peeled and
  chopped
2 red peppers, peeled, cored,
  deseeded and sliced
500ml hot chicken stock
  (see page 218)
2 tbsp chopped flat-leaf
  parsley

For the potatoes, preheat your oven to 180°C/Fan 165°C/Gas 4. Heat a frying pan large enough to take all the potatoes (or use two pans) over a medium-high heat, then add a drizzle of olive oil. When hot, add the onion, garlic and red peppers and fry for 4–5 minutes until starting to brown. Add the potato slices and fry for 2 minutes, adding a little more oil if needed.

Transfer the contents of the pan to an oven dish, pour on the hot chicken stock and season with salt and pepper. Bake for 30 minutes, or until the potatoes are tender.

In the meantime, light the barbecue 30 minutes before you plan to cook the fish.

Combine the olive oil and wine vinegar in a bottle or jar and give it a good shake.

When the coals are white hot, season the fish liberally with salt and place it in a large fish clamp. Put the fish on the barbecue and cook for a total of 15 minutes, turning and basting with the oil and vinegar mix every 2–3 minutes.

When the fish is nearly cooked, remove from the heat and allow it to rest for 10 minutes before eating. Serve the turbot whole on a warmed platter with the potatoes on the side.

Gurnard are fantastic for the barbecue. They love a good marinade and can handle bold flavours. I like to cook the small red species, but the bigger grey or tub gurnard is just as good. Try to avoid those with scales that seem impossible to remove – they are very sharp. The fennel salad is a lovely accompaniment, but you can serve what you like with the barbecued fish – or just eat them on their own with a squeeze of lemon, as I often do. Eating fish in this way allows you to really appreciate the difference between species, textures and tastes.

Gurnard with fennel, gherkin and olive salad

Serves 4
4 gurnard, 350–400g each
Sea salt and freshly ground
　black pepper

For the marinade
4 tsp fennel seeds
2 garlic cloves, peeled and
　finely chopped
4 tsp chopped thyme
2 tsp salt
100ml olive oil

**For the fennel, gherkin and
　olive salad**
2 banana shallots, peeled and
　thinly sliced
Finely grated zest and juice
　of 1 lemon
3 large gherkins, sliced
2 fennel bulbs, tough outer
　layer removed
100g black olives, pitted and
　sliced
2 tbsp fennel herb, roughly
　torn
100ml olive oil

For the marinade, toast the fennel seeds in a hot, dry pan for a couple of minutes until fragrant, then tip into a mortar and grind finely with the pestle. Add the garlic, thyme and salt and grind to a paste. Add the olive oil and mix well.

Score the gurnard several times on each side and rub all over with the marinade – be careful of the sharp bits! Leave to marinate in the fridge for at least an hour. Light your barbecue 30 minutes before you plan to start cooking, or preheat the grill to high.

To prepare the salad, put the shallots in a bowl with the lemon juice, sliced gherkins and a good pinch of salt. Toss to mix and leave to stand for 10 minutes.

Meanwhile, thinly slice the fennel, using a mandoline if you have one. Add the fennel, olives, lemon zest and fennel herb to the shallot mix and toss well. Dress with the olive oil. Taste for seasoning, adding more salt and a little pepper if you like.

When the coals are white hot, or the grill is ready, scrape off most of the marinade from the gurnard and carefully lay the fish on the barbecue grid or grill tray. Cook for 4 minutes on one side, then carefully turn the fish using a fish slice and cook for a further 4 minutes.

When the fish are cooked, carefully lift them onto a large platter. Serve straight away, with the salad on the side.

TO
FOLLOW

More like a French financier or madeleine than a traditional sponge, this is a versatile recipe that can take all manner of spices and pretty much any fruit. Rhubarb is one of my favourite fruits to bake and is delicious with the almond cream and sponge. All that richness and nuttiness is brought back to earth with the zingy crème fraîche. I like to serve these puddings warm from the oven, but you can let them cool down before eating if you prefer.

Rhubarb sponge, almond cream and lemon crème fraîche

Serves 8

For the sponge
2 vanilla pods, split
  lengthways
225g unsalted butter
225g egg whites (5–6 large)
225g caster sugar
90g ground almonds
90g plain flour
8 pieces of rhubarb, about
  10cm long

For the almond cream
90g ground almonds
65g caster sugar
300ml whole milk
1 vanilla pod, split lengthways

For the baked rhubarb
1kg rhubarb, cut into 8–10cm
  pieces
250g caster sugar
Zest and juice of 1 orange
  (zest microplaned)
100ml water

For the lemon crème fraîche
600ml full-fat crème fraîche
100g icing sugar
Grated zest and juice of
  1 lemon

Preheat your oven to 200°C/Fan 185°C/Gas 6. Line 8 individual moulds, about 8 x 4cm, with baking parchment.

To make the sponge, scrape the seeds from the vanilla pods and set aside. Put the pods into a saucepan with the butter and place over a medium heat. When the butter has melted and starts to brown, remove from the heat and allow to cool, then discard the vanilla pods.

Meanwhile, make the almond cream. Put the ground almonds, sugar and milk into a heavy-based pan with the vanilla. Place over a medium heat and cook, stirring often, until thickened; this will take about 15 minutes.

In the meantime, bake the rhubarb. Put the rhubarb, sugar, orange zest and juice, and the water into a deep roasting tray. Cook in the oven until the rhubarb is soft, about 10 minutes. Remove from the oven and leave to cool in the liquid.

When the almond cream is ready, remove from the heat, discard the vanilla pod and cover the surface with a disc of greaseproof paper to stop a skin forming.

To make the sponge, whisk the egg whites and sugar together in a large bowl for 1 minute. Add the ground almonds, flour and vanilla seeds and mix well. Finally, whisk in the brown butter, ensuring it is all incorporated. Pour the mixture into the prepared moulds. Lay the 8 rhubarb pieces on top of the mixture and bake for 12–14 minutes.

For the lemon crème fraîche, whisk the crème fraîche, icing sugar, lemon zest and juice together in a bowl. Cover and refrigerate until needed.

To check if the sponges are cooked, insert a small knife into the centre of one; if it comes out clean, it is ready. Turn out the sponges and place in shallow bowls. Serve warm with the baked rhubarb, almond cream and lemon crème fraîche.

Crumble has got to be one of the all-time favourite puddings. All that crunchy, slightly chewy topping with wonderful seasonal fruit underneath, served with lashings of custard, cream or ice cream – you can't go wrong... as long as you can make a good one. I like to cook this in individual dishes, but you can make a big crumble if you prefer. Any leftovers will reheat well too – I've even been known to have it for breakfast!

Pear crumble with Earl Grey chocolate sauce

Serves 4

For roasting
4 pears

For the pear compote
8 pears
50g unsalted butter
100ml pear cider
2 vanilla pods, split
  lengthways and seeds
  scraped

For the crumble mix
100g plain four
150g ground almonds
100g golden caster sugar
100g demerara sugar
100g unsalted butter, cut into
  small pieces

**For the Earl Grey chocolate
  sauce**
225ml double cream
100ml water
100g caster sugar
4 Earl Grey teabags
190g dark chocolate (70%
  cocoa solids), broken into
  small pieces

To make the chocolate sauce, put the cream, water and sugar into a pan and heat to dissolve the sugar, then bring to the boil. Add the teabags, take off the heat, cover and leave to infuse and cool.

Once cooled, strain the mixture into a clean pan. Bring to the boil, then remove from the heat. Immediately add the chocolate and whisk until smooth and shiny. Cover and set aside until ready to serve.

Preheat your oven to 180°C/Fan 165°C/Gas 4.

For the pear compote, peel, halve and core the pears, then cut into roughly equal sized chunks. Heat the butter and cider in a pan until the butter has melted. Add the vanilla seeds and stir well. Now add the pears and cook gently for 4 minutes. Divide the pear compote between individual baking dishes and set aside.

To make the crumble, mix the flour, ground almonds and sugars together in a bowl and rub in the butter with your fingertips or pulse in a food processor until the mixture looks like crumble.

Peel the pears for roasting and trim a thin slice from the base of each one, so they will stand upright.

Stand a pear in the centre of each baking dish. Scatter the crumble over the pear compote and bake for 25–30 minutes until golden and well cooked. When almost ready, gently warm the chocolate sauce.

Pour the warm chocolate sauce over the pears to serve.

To follow

In 2003, on the first menu of my first restaurant, Black Pig, I set about including a chocolate dessert that would be a lifelong friend. Over the years, in times of need, this recipe has saved the day and got me new friends! Of late, it has grown up and taken on a pastry jacket, making for a more interesting texture. I didn't want to share this recipe at first, because it's like a best friend, but having thought long and hard about it, I'd like you to reap the benefits too! I usually make individual tarts but you could bake one big one if you prefer.

Warm chocolate tart 'Black Pig'

Serves 6

For the pastry
430g plain flour, plus extra
  to dust
20g caster sugar
4g fine salt
4g baking powder
170g unsalted butter, softened
180ml milk (approximately)

For the chocolate filling
115g dark chocolate (70%
  cocoa solids), broken into
  small pieces
110g unsalted butter, softened
125g caster sugar
100g egg whites (about
  3 medium-large)
30g plain flour

To finish
Cocoa powder to dust

To make the pastry, mix all the dry ingredients together in a bowl. Using your fingers, rub in the butter until the mixture resembles a crumble mix. Add most of the milk and mix with a table knife to a smooth dough, adding as much of the remaining milk as you need, but don't overwork it. Place in a suitable plastic container with a lid and chill for 1 hour.

Preheat your oven to 180°C/Fan 165°C/Gas 4.

Unwrap the dough and roll out on a surface lightly dusted with flour to the thickness of a £1 coin. Cut out 6 circles and use to line 6 individual 8cm tart rings placed on a baking sheet, or use the sheet of pastry to line a 20cm tart tin. Place in the fridge to rest for 30 minutes.

Line the pastry case(s) with a double layer of greaseproof paper or aluminium foil and fill with baking beans. Pull the edges up and twist together to make little parcels in the tins. Bake for 15 minutes, then remove the baking bean parcel(s) and return the pastry case(s) to the oven for a further 5 minutes. When the pastry is cooked and golden, transfer the tart case(s) to a wire rack.

To make the chocolate filling, put the chocolate and butter into a large heatproof bowl over a pan of gently simmering water, making sure the base of the bowl is not touching the water. Leave until melted, then lift the bowl from the pan. Whisk the sugar into the chocolate mixture, then whisk in the egg whites. Finally, whisk in the flour until evenly combined.

Stand the tart case(s) on a baking tray and pour in the chocolate mixture, filling the case(s) to the top. Carefully transfer to the oven and bake for 10 minutes.

Serve straight from the oven dusted with cocoa powder, with a good dollop of clotted cream or ice cream of your choice on the side.

My good friend and chef, Pete Biggs, has been making this rice pudding for the restaurants for ages. I have to admit (through gritted teeth!) that his recipe is better than mine. Here, I'm serving it with my apple and prune compote, which is also lovely eaten simply with yoghurt. Do try it with this rice pudding though... the combination is seriously good.

Pete's rice pudding with apple and prune compote

Serves 6

For the compote
250g pitted prunes
100ml brandy
100ml water
100g caster sugar
Finely grated zest and juice
  of 1 lemon
½ cinnamon stick
1 vanilla pod, split lengthways
2 Bramley apples, peeled and
  diced

For the rice pudding
500ml whole milk
500ml double cream
½ tsp salt
2 vanilla pods, split
  lengthways and seeds
  scraped
150g pudding rice
90g caster sugar

To make the compote, soak the prunes in the brandy overnight. The following day, heat the water and sugar in a saucepan to dissolve the sugar, then bring to the boil. Add the lemon zest and juice, cinnamon stick and vanilla pod. Simmer for 2 minutes, then add the prunes and any remaining brandy. Bring back to a simmer and take off the heat.

Leave until cold and then transfer the prunes, flavourings and liquor to a sterilised Kilner jar. Seal and store in a cool, dark place; the longer the prunes have to mature (up to a month), the better they will be. Leave them for at least 4 or 5 days if you can.

For the rice pudding, preheat your oven to 160°C/Fan 145°C/ Gas 3. Put all the ingredients into a large ovenproof pan, including the vanilla pods as well as the seeds, and stir well. Bring to a simmer over a medium heat and then take off the heat. Lay a circle of greaseproof paper on the surface and transfer to the oven to cook for 30 minutes.

In the meantime, put the prune compote into a pan and add the diced apples. Stir and bring to a simmer over a low heat. Cook for a couple of minutes until the apples are just tender.

To serve, I like to put the pan of rice pudding in the centre of the table with the bowl of apple and prune compote on the side and let everyone help themselves.

Make this dessert at the beginning of the summer, when British strawberries are amazing and the hedgerows are full of elderflower. There is a bit of time involved here but believe me, it's worth it. The sweeter the strawberries, the better it will be. The set cream and sorbet recipes are versatile, so feel free to play around with the flavours.

Elderflower cream with strawberry sorbet

Serves 6

For the elderflower cream
2 sheets of bronze leaf
  gelatine
560ml whole milk
180ml double cream
90g caster sugar
100ml elderflower cordial

For the strawberry sorbet
500g strawberries
500ml sparkling wine
250g caster sugar

To finish
15 strawberries, hulled and
  quartered
Finely grated zest of 1 lime

Mix together all the ingredients for the strawberry sorbet in a pan. Set over a medium heat and bring to a simmer. Simmer gently until the strawberries are soft. Cool slightly and put into a blender. Blitz until smooth, then pass through a sieve to remove any pips. Place in an ice-cream machine and churn until frozen. Alternatively, pour into a suitable plastic container and place in the freezer, stirring every half hour until frozen. (This will give a granita-like consistency.)

To make the elderflower cream, soak the gelatine in a shallow dish of ice-cold water. Pour the milk and cream into a pan, add the sugar and dissolve over a medium heat, then bring to a simmer and take off the heat. Immediately drain the gelatine and add to the hot milk mixture, whisking until melted, then whisk in the elderflower cordial.

Pour the elderflower cream into 6 individual dishes or glasses, dividing the mixture evenly, and place in the fridge to set for 3 hours.

To assemble, gently toss the quartered strawberries with the lime zest and spoon on top of the elderflower creams. Using a warmed ice-cream scoop or large spoon, scoop balls of the sorbet and place on top of the strawberries and cream. Serve immediately.

My daughter, Jessica, loves to bake. Ever since I can remember, she's joined me in the kitchen at home. Of all her baking successes (and there have been many), this is the recipe that to date is the family's favourite. Why 'Messie'? Well, in all my years of cooking, I've never seen anyone more accomplished in getting every surface in the kitchen and herself covered in whatever she's making. We 'borrowed' this recipe from Claire Clark, my friend and the world's best pastry chef.

Messie Jessie cookies

Makes 10

150g unsalted butter, at room
   temperature
80g soft light brown sugar
80g granulated sugar
A pinch of sea salt
½ tsp vanilla extract
1 medium egg
250g plain flour
½ tsp bicarbonate of soda
100g dark chocolate (70%
   cocoa solids), chopped
100g milk chocolate, chopped

Using an electric mixer, beat the butter, sugars, salt and vanilla extract together until thoroughly combined. Add the egg and beat in well.

Sift the flour and bicarbonate of soda over the mixture and mix until evenly combined. Finally, fold in the dark and milk chocolate buttons.

Form the dough into a log, wrap in greaseproof paper, twisting the ends to secure, then place in the fridge for 3 hours to firm up.

Preheat your oven to 170°C/Fan 155°C/Gas 3½. Line 2 baking trays with baking parchment.

Divide the dough into 10 equal pieces and shape into balls. Place on the baking trays, leaving enough room in between for spreading. Bake for 15–20 minutes until golden.

Leave the cookies on the trays for a minute or two to firm up slightly, then transfer to a wire rack and leave to cool – that is if you can resist eating them straight away.

I find meringues fascinating – the fact that simple egg whites and sugar can be whisked together to create something so special is magic, and I always have some sort of meringue dessert on my restaurant menus. I like to balance the sweetness with something sharp, hence the lemon and tangy yoghurt sorbet topping for this pavlova. It's a favourite dessert at home.

Lemon curd pavlova with yoghurt sorbet

Serves 6

For the meringue
3 medium egg whites
150g caster sugar
1 vanilla pod, split lengthways
 and seeds scraped
2 tsp cornflour
2 tsp white wine vinegar

For the lemon curd
Finely grated zest of 1 lemon
130ml lemon juice (about
 3 lemons)
100g caster sugar
80g egg yolks (about
 4 medium)
1 egg white
200g unsalted butter, chilled
 and diced

For the yoghurt sorbet
200ml whole milk
100g caster sugar
120ml liquid glucose
300g full-fat Greek yoghurt

For the lemon syrup
200ml liquid glucose
Finely grated zest of 1 lemon
100ml lemon juice
100g caster sugar

To finish
50g flaked almonds, toasted

Preheat your oven to 110°C/Gas ¼ and line a baking sheet with a silicone mat or baking parchment. Wipe your stand mixer (or other large) bowl with kitchen paper dipped in vinegar to remove any trace of grease.

Using a stand mixer or electric hand mixer, whisk the egg whites in the bowl to soft peaks. Whisk in the sugar a third at a time until fully incorporated; add the vanilla seeds with the last of the sugar. Gently fold in the cornflour and wine vinegar, using a spatula or large metal spoon.

Using a large spoon, shape the meringue into 6 equal sized mounds on the prepared tray and then use the back of the spoon to make an indent in each one. Bake the meringues for 1 hour.

Meanwhile, make the lemon curd. Whisk the lemon zest and juice, sugar, egg yolks and egg white in a heatproof bowl over a pan of simmering water until the mixture thickens. Remove the bowl from the pan and whisk in the cold butter, a piece at a time, until it is all incorporated. Strain through a sieve into a bowl, cover and refrigerate until set.

To make the yoghurt sorbet, put the milk, sugar and liquid glucose into a pan and place over a medium heat to dissolve the sugar. Bring to a simmer, take off the heat and leave to cool. Once cold, whisk in the yoghurt, then transfer to an ice-cream machine and churn until thick.

For the lemon syrup, heat the glucose, lemon zest and juice, and the sugar in a pan over a medium heat to dissolve the sugar. Let simmer for 3 minutes, then pour the syrup into a bowl and leave to cool.

When the sorbet is ready, spoon into a suitable container and place in the freezer. When the meringues are cooked, transfer to a wire rack to cool.

To assemble, put a spoonful of lemon curd in the centre of each bowl and place a meringue on top. Drizzle the lemon syrup over the meringues and around each plate. Top each meringue with a scoop of the sorbet. Scatter over the toasted almonds and serve, with an extra spoonful of lemon curd on the side, if you like.

I know a lot of people find treacle tart overly sweet. My filling includes black treacle, salt and citrus flavours to take the edge off the sweetness, and the raspberries balance the flavours beautifully. You can have ice cream with it if you like but, for me, it has to be clotted or pouring cream. It's easier to make a larger quantity of pastry and it freezes well – so I've given enough here to make two tarts.

Treacle and raspberry tart

Serves 6

For the sweet pastry
200g unsalted butter, diced
180g icing sugar
1 medium egg
140g egg yolks (about
  6 large)
500g plain flour, plus extra
  to dust

For the filling
225g golden syrup
50g black treacle
220ml double cream
½ tsp coarse sea salt
Finely grated zest of 1 orange
Finely grated zest of 1 lemon
Juice of ½ lemon
75g fresh white breadcrumbs
2 medium eggs, beaten
100g raspberries, plus extra
  to serve

To make the pastry, using a stand mixer or electric hand whisk, cream the butter and icing sugar together in a bowl until pale and fluffy. Lightly beat the egg and egg yolks in a separate bowl. Gradually beat the egg into the creamed mixture. Once it is all incorporated, add the flour. Stop mixing as soon as it forms a dough.

Tip the dough out onto a surface dusted lightly with flour and knead briefly until smooth. Divide in half, shape each piece into a ball and flatten to a disc. Wrap in greaseproof paper or place in a suitable plastic container. Chill one portion in the fridge for 1 hour; freeze the other for another tart.

Preheat your oven to 180°C/Fan 165°C/Gas 4.

Roll out the pastry on a lightly floured surface to the thickness of a £1 coin and use to line a loose-based rectangular flan tin, about 25 x 10cm and 3cm deep, or an 18cm round flan tin, 3cm deep, leaving any excess overhanging the rim. Place in the fridge to rest for 30 minutes.

Line the pastry case with a double layer of greaseproof paper or aluminium foil and fill with baking beans. Pull the edges up and twist together to make a parcel. Bake for 15 minutes, then remove the baking bean parcel and return the pastry case to the oven for a further 5 minutes until golden and cooked. Place on a wire rack to cool.

To make the filling, put the golden syrup, treacle, cream, salt, citrus zests and lemon juice into a heavy-based pan and stir over a medium heat until the mixture is smooth and very hot. Take the pan off the heat and add the breadcrumbs and beaten eggs. Mix until evenly combined.

Spoon the filling into the pastry case and add the raspberries, distributing them evenly. Bake for 15 minutes, until the filling is just set in the centre. Place on a wire rack to cool, trimming away the excess pastry from the rim while the tart is still just warm.

Cut the tart into slices and serve just warm or at room temperature, with extra raspberries on the side and clotted cream or pouring cream.

This recipe is inspired by nostalgic memories of ice-cream sandwiches my Mum would make with Neapolitan ice cream bought from the ice-cream man. I'd like to think my take is an improvement!

Passion fruit and toasted coconut ice-cream sandwich

Serves 6

For the ice cream
300ml fresh passion fruit juice (from about 20 passion fruit)
3 sheets of bronze leaf gelatine
400ml double cream
5 medium egg yolks
120g caster sugar
260g full-fat cream cheese, at room temperature

For the coconut biscuit
55g desiccated coconut
100g egg whites (about 3 medium)
100g caster sugar
100g plain flour

For the coconut yoghurt
50g desiccated coconut
300g full-fat Greek yoghurt
Finely grated zest of 1 lime
30g icing sugar

For the passion fruit syrup
80ml passion fruit pulp (from about 4 scooped-out passion fruit)
50g caster sugar

For the ice cream, pour the passion fruit juice into a large pan and bring to a simmer over a medium heat. Let bubble to reduce by three-quarters, then take off the heat. Soak the gelatine in a dish of ice-cold water.

Add the cream to the reduced passion fruit juice and return to a simmer. Meanwhile, whisk the egg yolks and sugar together in a bowl. Pour on the hot passion fruit cream, whisking as you do so. While it is still very hot, squeeze the excess water from the gelatine, then add to the mixture, whisking to melt completely. Let cool, then cover and refrigerate until set.

Once the mixture is cold, whisk in the cream cheese. Spoon into a piping bag and pipe into 6 individual rectangular moulds. Freeze until firm.

To make the biscuit, preheat your oven to 180°C/Fan 165°C/Gas 4 and the grill to medium-high. Scatter the desiccated coconut on a grill tray and grill until golden, stirring every 2 minutes to colour evenly. Let cool.

Line a baking tray with a silicone mat. Whisk the egg whites and sugar together in a bowl until evenly mixed. Add the toasted coconut and flour and stir to combine. Using a palette knife, spread the mixture thinly and evenly on the baking tray. Bake for 8–10 minutes until golden all over.

When you take the tray from the oven, mark your desired biscuit shapes with a sharp knife. Once cooled, they should snap where marked, with a little help. Keep in an airtight container until ready to assemble.

For the coconut yoghurt, toast the coconut as above and let cool. Once cooled, add to the yoghurt with the lime zest and icing sugar and stir until evenly combined. Set aside in the fridge until ready to serve.

For the syrup, heat the passion fruit pulp and sugar in a pan over a medium heat to dissolve the sugar. Bring to a simmer, lower the heat slightly and cook until reduced to a syrupy consistency. Leave to cool.

To assemble, unmould the ice creams and sandwich each one between two coconut biscuits. Serve immediately, with the passion fruit syrup spooned over and a dollop of coconut yoghurt on the side.

BASICS

Lemon oil

Makes about 400ml

Finely pared zest of
 5 unwaxed lemons
300ml light rapeseed oil
100ml light olive oil

Put the pared zest of 4 lemons into a blender with the oils and blitz for 2 minutes. Pour the oil mixture into a jug and leave to infuse and settle for 24 hours. Decant the oil into a sterilised bottle and add the pared zest of the remaining lemon. Keep in the fridge and use within a month.

Horseradish and lemon oil Add 75g grated fresh horseradish to the blender with the other ingredients.

Orange oil

Makes about 400ml

Finely pared zest of 4 oranges
300ml light rapeseed oil
100ml light olive oil

Put all of the ingredients into a blender and blitz for 2 minutes. Pour the oil mixture into a jug and leave to infuse and settle for 24 hours. Decant the oil into a sterilised bottle. Keep in the fridge and use within a month.

Basil oil

Makes about 150ml

30g basil leaves
30g flat-leaf parsley leaves
150ml light olive oil
Cornish sea salt

Bring a pan of salted water to a simmer and get a bowl of iced water ready. When the water is simmering, add the herbs and blanch for 30 seconds. Immediately scoop out the herbs and plunge them straight into the iced water to cool quickly. Drain and squeeze out excess water.

Put the blanched herbs into a blender with the olive oil and blitz for 2 minutes. Transfer the mixture to a container, cover and refrigerate for at least 3–4 hours, preferably overnight.

Warm the oil slightly, then pass it through a sieve into a clean bottle. The oil is now ready to use. It will keep in the fridge for a week.

Chilli oil

Makes about 400ml

2 green chillies, chopped
 (seeds left in)
400ml light rapeseed oil

Put the chillies and oil into a saucepan. Warm over a medium heat – until the oil is just too hot to put your finger in. Remove from the heat and pour the oil and chillies into a food processor. Blend for 2 minutes, then pour the liquid into a container and leave to cool.

Once cold, strain the oil into a clean bottle and store in the fridge until needed. It will keep in the fridge for a week.

Curry oil

Makes about 400ml

4 tsp mild curry powder
400ml light rapeseed oil

Sprinkle the curry powder into a dry frying pan and toast over a medium heat for 1–2 minutes until it releases its aroma; don't let it burn. Pour the oil into the frying pan and immediately remove from the heat. Give it a good stir and then pour it into a jug.

Leave to infuse and settle for 24 hours, then decant the curry oil into a sterilised bottle. It will keep for 3 months in a dark cupboard.

Fish stock

Makes about 500ml

1kg turbot, brill or sole bones
and/or cod heads, washed
and all blood removed

Preheat your oven to 200°C/Fan 185°C/Gas 6. Line a roasting tray with silicone paper and lay the fish bones and/or cod heads in it. Roast for 30 minutes, then turn the bones over and roast for another 10 minutes.

Transfer the roasted bones to a stockpot and pour on enough water to cover. Bring to a simmer over a medium heat and skim off any impurities from the surface. Simmer for 30 minutes, then take off the heat and strain through a sieve into another pan. Bring the stock back to a simmer and reduce by half. Remove from the heat and allow to cool.

The stock is now ready to use. You can store it in the fridge for up to 3 days or freeze it for up to 2 months.

Chicken stock

Makes about 500ml

2kg chicken bones

Preheat your oven to 200°C/Fan 185°C/Gas 6. Place all the bones in a roasting tray and roast for 30 minutes, then turn them over and roast for another 30 minutes.

Transfer the bones to a stockpot and cover with water. Bring to the boil and simmer for 3 hours, skimming the surface regularly. Pass the stock through a sieve into another pan. Bring back to a simmer and reduce by half. Remove from the heat and allow to cool.

The stock is now ready to use. You can store it in the fridge for up to 3 days or freeze it for up to 2 months.

Vegetable stock

Makes about 2 litres

2 onions, peeled and finely
chopped
6 carrots, peeled and finely
chopped
6 celery sticks, finely chopped
2 leeks, trimmed, washed and
finely sliced
2 garlic cloves, peeled and
crushed
10 white peppercorns
2 star anise
2 tsp fennel seeds
Pinch of sea salt
500ml dry white wine
1 thyme sprig
A handful of parsley stalks

Put all of the vegetables, the garlic, spices and salt into a large saucepan and pour on enough water to cover. Bring to a simmer over a medium heat. Simmer for 30 minutes and then remove from the heat. Pour the wine into the stock and add the herbs. Leave to cool.

For best results, leave overnight in the fridge before straining the stock to remove the vegetables, spices and herbs. The stock is now ready to use. It can be frozen for up to 2 months.

Mayonnaise

Makes about 350ml

3 egg yolks
1 tsp English mustard
Juice of ½ lemon, or 2 tsp
  white wine vinegar or cider
  vinegar
300ml light rapeseed oil
Sea salt and freshly ground
  black pepper

Put the egg yolks, mustard and lemon juice or wine (or cider) vinegar into a bowl and whisk together for 1 minute. Now slowly add the oil, drop by drop to begin with, then in a thin, steady stream, whisking constantly, until the mixture is emulsified and thick. (Or you can make the mayonnaise in a blender or food processor, blending the egg yolks, mustard and lemon juice or vinegar for 1 minute and then adding the oil in a thin, steady stream through the funnel with the motor running.)

Season the mayonnaise with salt and pepper to taste. Cover and refrigerate until needed. It will keep in the fridge for a couple of days.

Herb mayonnaise Add 3–4 tbsp chopped herbs to the finished mayonnaise. Dill, tarragon and parsley are good options with fish.

Spicy anchovy mayonnaise Put 2 egg yolks, a pinch of saffron strands, 2 chopped garlic cloves, 1 finely chopped deseeded chilli, 4 salted anchovies in oil and the juice of ½ lemon into a blender or small food processor and blitz for 1 minute. With the motor running, slowly add 400ml olive oil through the funnel. Season the mayonnaise, scrape into a bowl, cover and refrigerate as above.

Tomato ketchup

Makes 400ml; serves 10–12

A drizzle of olive oil
2 red onions, peeled and
  chopped
6 garlic cloves, peeled and
  sliced
20 black peppercorns
2.5kg ripe tomatoes, roughly
  chopped
100g caster sugar
4 tsp chopped thyme
1 cinnamon stick
4 bay leaves
300ml red wine vinegar
Sea salt and freshly ground
  black pepper

Heat a large saucepan over a medium heat and add the olive oil. When hot, add the onions and garlic and cook for 2 minutes until the onions start to turn translucent.

Meanwhile, tie the peppercorns in a piece of muslin and add to the pan with the tomatoes, sugar, thyme, cinnamon and bay leaves. Cook for 15 minutes until the tomatoes have broken down. Continue to cook until the tomato liquid has reduced right down, almost to nothing. Now add the wine vinegar and let bubble for 5 minutes.

Remove the cinnamon, bay and peppercorn bundle. Tip the contents of the pan into a blender or food processor and blend until smooth, then pass though a sieve into a bowl. Taste for seasoning, adding salt and pepper as required.

Transfer to a clean container and allow to cool, then seal. The tomato ketchup will keep in the fridge for up to a week; or you can freeze it for up to a month.

Index

Dedication

This book is dedicated to Joseph Tyers, a talented young chef who was taken too early from our stoves but lives on in our kitchens. Joe, you will never be forgotten. X

Acknowledgements

I genuinely feel like the luckiest chef alive. The family that surrounds me is the reason I am here and allowed me the time to write this book.

Rachel, as always my rock and my best friend. Love you Chicken!

Jacob and Jessica, my now not-so-little monkeys, I love you too.

And Bud, the Lurcher, who is still making me smile, whatever time of the day or night along with new addition to the family, George.

Dad, thanks for being Dad.

Mum, thanks for typing all my scribbles and decoding my writing. I couldn't have done it without you.

Ashley Outlaw, thanks for helping with the prep!

Chris Simpson, thank you for all your support and friendship. Your help with this book has been invaluable.

Pete Biggs, my right-hand man for so long now. There are no words.

Tim Barnes, always there, pushing on and helping. Cheers!

Stephi and Damon Little, your loyalty and support is always appreciated.

Ian Dodgson and Anna Davey. You two are 'strong'! The help and support you give me is amazing. Thank you.

Karl Lucking, thanks for all your hard work front of house.

Emma Meech, for everything you do to make things run smoothly.

The teams at Restaurant Nathan Outlaw/Outlaw's New Road and Outlaw's Fish Kitchen, you know who you are! Thanks for all your hard work over the years.

To David Hunter (spreadsheets and numbers), Chris Prindl (pots and crockery) and Danny Madigan (you name it, he does it!) my thanks for all your particular skills. You've been amazing.

At Quadrille, thanks to Helen Lewis for the creative vision and on-going support on the third book together.

To my editor, Janet Illsley, who must think I don't know what the word 'deadline' means... sorry, but a massive thanks!

David Loftus, for once again making my food look fantastic with his camera. It's such an honour to work with you.

Jamie Oliver, thank you from the bottom of my heart for writing such a lovely foreword. It means so much.

And a final thanks to you for buying, borrowing or stealing this book! I hope it brings you lots of fun...

Publishing director Sarah Lavelle
Creative director Helen Lewis
Project editor Janet Illsley
Design concept and illustration Arielle Gamble
Designer Emily Lapworth
Photography David Loftus
Food for photography Nathan Outlaw
Production Emily Noto, Vincent Smith

First published in 2016. This edition published in 2021 by Quadrille, an imprint of Hardie Grant Publishing quadrille.com

Cataloguing in Publication Data: a catalogue record for this book is available from the British Library.

ISBN 9781787138339

Printed in China